The
Bare-Bottomed
Skier

Other books by Jerry Bledsoe

*The World's Number One, Flat-Out, All-Time-Great Stock
Car Racing Book (1975)*
You Can't Live On Radishes (1976)
Just Folks (1980)
Where's Mark Twain When We Really Need Him? (1981)
Carolina Curiosities (1984)
From Whalebone to Hothouse (1986)
Bitter Blood (1988)
Country Cured (1989)
North Carolina Curiosities (1990)

The Bare-Bottomed Skier

And Other Unlikely Tales

By Jerry Bledsoe

Illustrated by Tim Rickard

 Down Home Press • Asheboro, N.C.

ISBN 0-9624255-8-3

Library of Congress Catalog Card Number 90-062192

Printed in the United States of America

Cover design by Harry Blair
Book design by Elizabeth House

Much of the material in this book
originally appeared, some in slightly different form,
in the *Greensboro News & Record.*
It was compiled and edited by Erik Bledsoe

Down Home Press
P.O. Box 4126
Asheboro, N.C. 27204

For
Goof
&
The Little Girl,
to whom
I always can turn for laughter.

Contents

Doing My Civic Duties

Awards and Honors

I Read It In The Newspaper

Preachers, Parties and Other Particulars

The Agony of Victory

Only In The South

From Giant Collards to Frustrated Flamingos

An Elephant
Stepped on my Car

The Bare-Bottomed Skier

For twenty-three years, I wrote regular newspaper columns. First for the *Greensboro Daily News*. Then for the *Charlotte Observer*. Finally back again in Greensboro for the *News & Record*. (I tended to have trouble with editors, thus prompting moves, sometimes on short notice.) During that time, I managed to provoke a lot of response from readers.

Much of this response was predictable. All columnists know that some subjects are certain to bring reaction. Attack cats, Jesse Helms, slick TV preachers or Elvis, and you know that you will be busy on the phone for days, and the hate mail will pile up on your desk. Sometimes the trouble of all this isn't worth the easy extra column or two that you get from it.

During my long career of reveling in such shenanigans, three columns stand out for the sheer volume of response that they brought. One was a take-off on a sixties' group of teeny-bopper idols called the Monkees. Another was from the same era: a defense of long hair on males. And the third was when I became the very first person to reveal that Elvis was still alive, years before others began spotting him at Dairy Queens and bowling alleys and other hot spots. All brought avalanches of calls and mail, most of it nasty.

Response of that sort is better than no response at all, of course, (going unnoticed is the worst fate that can befall a columnist) but it does not necessarily translate to love or popularity, which is what the average columnist longs for most.

I also was fortunate to write some columns that proved very popular, although the beloved columns never brought anywhere near the quantity of response that the hated ones provoked.

3

One of these columns brought far more reaction than any others. That was the one about the bare-bottomed skier. It appeared in the *Greensboro News & Record* in March of 1982, and not a year has passed since that I have not received mail or calls about it, most asking for copies. The demand for copies was so great that for years I kept a stack of photo copies on my desk to mail out. One man wrote to tell me that he had carried a copy of the column in his lunch box for years so that he could take it out and chuckle over it now and then, or read it to to fellow workers. It finally had become so besmudged by grease spots, soup spills and coffee stains that he couldn't read it any more, and he didn't know how he could continue to get through the work day without the knowledge that a readable copy of the plight of the bare-bottomed skier was keeping the bottom of his lunch box from being bare. Some of those who wrote or called about the column even requested that I include it in a book someday. For those, the long wait is over. Herewith, once again, is the tale of the bare-bottomed skier:

It is supposed to be a true story, and since it was sent to me by a minister, who, at his request, shall be nameless, surely it must be so.

It happened at a North Carolina ski resort, which one he's not exactly certain. He, alas, did not witness the incident himself.

She was a good skier, and with private instruction she had moved quickly to advanced classes. She and her instructor had gone to the top of a difficult slope for a trial run, but before they could begin, the young woman felt an overwhelming call of nature.

Going back to the lodge was not feasible, so she decided to ski to a nearby laurel thicket to seek relief. She had just finished with the embarrassing intrusion and was about to stand and retrieve the affected apparel from about her ankles when her skis began to move. She made a desperate grab for her clothes — but succeeded only in launching herself into full motion.

It was too late to think about clothes because she had to concentrate on dodging trees and bushes. Somehow she managed it and shot onto the slope, gathering momentum, still in her awkward position.

She tried to stand but couldn't because of the clothing entangling her knees. With her speed quickening dramatically, she tried to snowplow to a stop but the clothing kept her from getting her feet in the right position.

Fearful now, she saw ahead what appeared to be a snowbank and decided her only chance to stop was to plow right into it. Instead of stopping her it merely catapulted her onto the main slope.

She slalomed around a light post, past a group of startled skiers and headed for the base of the mountain picking up speed and shouting at skiers in her path. In near panic she thought of trying to stop by simply sitting down, but she remembered her exposed condition, quickly evaluated the consequences, and reconsidered.

A member of the ski patrol took up her chase, and her instructor appeared, far behind, trying to catch up.

Some said that when she passed the lodge she appeared to be going well over 60 miles per hour. Behind her was a trail littered with gaping skiers in various states of disarray, most of them still not quite believing what they'd just seen.

She careened onto the beginners' slope, which flattened at the bottom and turned uphill, and made her way well up the hill before she finally came to a stop.

The member of the ski patrol was first to

reach her. She was exhausted, appeared to be in shock, was suffering severe leg cramps and just a touch of frostbite. The ski patrol member bundled her in a blanket and carried her to a first aid station.

She was admitted to the hospital for over-night observation and morning found her fit, though still embarrassed.

As she was leaving the hospital, she en-countered a young man, also leaving, wearing casts on both arms and a bandage around his head. She noticed his ski attire and asked what happened.

"You'd never believe it," he said. "I was skiing yesterday when I heard something behind me. I turned around and saw this scream-ing woman headed straight for me. She was hunkered down, had her pants down around her ankles and was waving like crazy. I tried to get out of her way and skied into a tree. Broke both arms and my nose."

I knew the story wasn't true, of course. By that stage in my career, I recognized such stories immediately. Heaven knows I had encountered enough of them. The stories even had been categorized with a name and were the subject of study by sociologists. "Urban tales," they were called, although they often had rural settings. Nobody knew where they came from, but they spread from mouth to mouth, city to city, all over the country, some of them horror stories, some of them humorous.

The first such story that I recall spread through my hometown, Thomasville, N.C., when I was in high school there back in the '50s. I don't remember the details of it now, but it was a funny story about a fellow called Ski King, and it was supposed to have happened at High Rock Lake, right there in Davidson County. We all accepted it as the gospel truth and were delighted when a popular record about Ski King hit the the radio stations, because we thought that something that

6

happened in our own county had been recognized nationally. Only later did we learn that the Ski King story had spread through hundreds of similar towns, and in each town it had happened at a nearby lake. I never was certain whether the promoters of the record started that story, or whether they merely capitalized on it. My guess would be the latter.

These stories have to start somewhere, of course, but tracing them to their origins is almost impossible. They spread rapidly, and with each telling, the location is apt to change. The identity of the people in the stories usually is vague, the friend of a friend, or somebody that a neighbor worked with, or went to school with. Sometimes, the people are never really identified, and only the location of the story is important.

The first such story that I recall using in my column was the one about the dead cat. It was a location story. I first read it in a Danville, Va., newspaper. The newspaper reported that the story was supposed to be true and that it had happened in Danville, but the participants weren't identified. Here's that one:

A man and his wife were driving into town on a shopping trip when a big yellow cat ran in front of their car. The man tried to miss it, but couldn't.

He stopped to check on the cat and found that he had killed it. There was a house nearby, so he went over and knocked on the door and asked the woman who answered if she owned a yellow cat.

"Yes, why?"

"I'm sorry," he said, "but I think I ran over your cat. It ran in front of the car. I couldn't help it. It's dead. I'm sorry."

The woman was obviously upset, and the man didn't know what to do.

"Could I pay for the cat?" he asked. "Or buy you another one?"

"No," she said, brushing back tears. "It's

not your fault. I shouldn't have let him out of the house. I knew it was going to happen someday. He just wouldn't keep away from that road."

"I wish there was something I could do," the man persisted.

"Well," said the woman. "There is one thing. I don't think I could stand to bury him. Would you mind disposing of him for me?"

Certainly, said the man. He would be glad to. It was the least he could do. So he fetched the cat from the road, put it into a shopping bag that he had in his car, and he and his wife continued on to the shopping center, planning to bury the cat when they returned home.

At the shopping center, the man got to thinking that the dead cat might smell up the closed car, so he set the shopping bag beside the car until he and his wife had finished their errands. They were on their way back to the parking lot when they noticed a woman walk over to their car, glance furtively about, snatch up the shopping bag and hurry off.

The man and his wife were so amused by this that they decided to follow the woman and see her reaction when she looked into the bag and realized what she had stolen. The woman went into a department store, made her way to the lunch counter, perched herself on a stool and stole a little peek into the bag. She gasped, let out a little moan and fainted dead away, toppling from the stool and striking her head.

Several people gathered around. Somebody called an ambulance. She was still out when it arrived. The EMTs worked to revive her, and when she began to come around, they loaded her onto a stretcher, covered her with a sheet and began wheeling her out.

"Wait a minute," called a waitress hurrying after them. "This is her shopping bag."

The EMTs took it, placed it on her belly, and away they went.

After I used that story, I started getting calls from people who also had heard the story. The Danville paper was wrong, they said, because the story had happened in Greensboro, at Friendly Center, and they knew somebody who knew somebody who had been there and had seen it for themselves, although they couldn't actually identify the people involved. Later, I read the same story in the Asheville newspaper, which reported it to be true, and that it had happened right in Asheville. For years afterward, I still kept seeing the story in other newspapers, all dutifully reporting that it had happened in their towns. After that, I was always wary of such tales.

When the one about the woman and the elephant turned up, for example, it was supposed to have happened in Reidsville to a friend of a friend. A few calls was all it took to convince me that it hadn't happened in Reidsville and probably never happened at all, but it was a good story, and I used it, although I never maintained that it was true, or that it was supposed to have occurred anywhere in the vicinity.

A hefty woman enrolled in one of those weight reduction programs and trimmed down to about half her former size. To celebrate, she went out and bought a tiny, shiny, red sports car, just to prove that she could fit in it.

On the very day she bought the car, she stopped at a shopping center where a small carnival was setting up in a corner of the parking lot. She went into a department store to shop for some dashing new clothes to go with her new, trim figure and flashy, new car. After leaving the department store, she hurried over to the nearby supermarket to pick up a few things for supper, then started for her car.

She gasped when she spotted it. There were big dents in the roof, the hood, the trunk. The fenders were smashed.

She was staring at her car in disbelief when a man hurried over and introduced himself as the owner of the carnival that was setting up in the parking lot. He explained that an elephant performed with the carnival. It had pulled free from its tether and escaped. Before anybody noticed it was gone, it had mistaken her car for the red stand that it used in its act and had rehearsed all over it. The man was very apologetic. He gave her his card, the name and number of his insurance company. He would take care of all damages, he said. He was sure the car could be fixed as good as new.

The woman was distraught, of course, but what could she do? Although battered, her car would run still. She could drive it. So she got in and started home with a tale to tell. On the way, she came upon a very bad wreck that had just happened. Several cars were involved and they were strewn all over the road. She saw that people were hurt, and having had first aid training, she stopped and got out to see if she could help.

Police and ambulances soon arrived, and seeing that help was now at hand and she had done all she could, the woman got back into her car and started to leave.

"Wait a minute," called a policeman, who just had begun surveying the scene, trying to figure out what had happened. "Where do you think you're going?"

"I just didn't think I was needed anymore, so I was going on home," the woman said.

"Don't you know you can't leave the scene of an accident?" the police officer said.

"Oh, I wasn't involved in the accident," the woman said, but she realized that the policeman was walking around her bashed car, checking it carefully, and she could see that he didn't believe her.

"I think you'd better get out and let me see your driver's license," the policeman said. "I think you've got a little explaining to do."

"Oh, I can explain," the woman said cheerily. "I saw this wreck and I just stopped to see if I could help. I wasn't in the wreck. See, an elephant stepped on my car a little while ago."

"Sure, lady," said the policeman. "That's what they all say."

"No, that's the truth," protested the woman. "An elephant stepped on my car. I can prove it. See, he thought it was his stand, and...."

"I think you'd better come with me," the officer said, taking her by the arm.

"No, I can't go," she cried. "I've got frozen stuff in my groceries. I wasn't involved in this, I'm telling you. An elephant stepped on my car."

"Sure, sure," the officer said consolingly, as he led her away, she protesting loudly with every step.

Before she knew what was happening, he had opened the back of an ambulance and was stuffing her in with several victims from the accident.

"Here's another one," he told the EMT who was attending the others. "See that they check this one for head injuries."

As unlikely as that story is, it was no more unlikely than the one about the two elderly women in New York. This one was unusual in that it came connected with an actual name, a device that made it seem all the more believable. It was supposed to have happened to a matron from a prominent Greensboro family. A single call was all I needed to find out that she knew nothing about it. Everywhere that it was told – and it swept the nation – it was told with the name of a prominent local woman connected to it. It also was widely reported by newspapers as a true story, and it even made the august *New York Times*.

The story was that this woman had decided she wanted to go to New York to see some plays. Her family, thinking about all the crime in the city, was reluctant to let her go.

But she was insistent, and her family finally relented on the condition she take along a companion. She chose a friend about her own age.

The two women flew to New York, caught a taxi into Manhattan and checked into an upper-floor room at the Plaza Hotel, a snazzy place. Although they had promised their families that they would be cautious and wouldn't go out any more than necessary, they decided to walk to a nice, nearby restaurant for dinner.

When they got onto the elevator on their floor, the elevator was empty. They started down, but the elevator stopped after a few floors. The doors opened and there stood a hulking man holding the leashes on two big Doberman pinschers.

The women paled and shrank against the back of the elevator as the man and dogs entered. The man turned to face the door.

"Sit," he commanded.

His dogs – and both ladies – sat.

The man didn't notice the women hunkered, quaking, behind him until the elevator landed and he saw the shocked expressions of the people waiting in the lobby to get on. The women, seeing open spaces, gathered themselves up, scurried from the elevator and fled the hotel on the run.

They each downed a couple of stiff drinks at the restaurant before they were able to overcome their fright and embarrassment and proceed with dinner.

After they'd eaten and called for the check, the waiter informed them that their bill had been paid.

"Mr. Reggie Jackson asked me to tell you that he hoped you enjoyed your dinner and that he and his dogs apologize for frightening you," the waiter said.

All of these stories brought response from readers, but nothing to compare with that which eventually came from the tale of the bare-bottomed skier. I'll have to admit that I never quite understood the overwhelming popularity of that story. It's amusing enough, but not as funny, I think, as many other columns I wrote. And that has always been a little troubling to me, I guess. In all those years of column writing, I always struggled to be clever and original, to write columns that were funny, or biting or touching. And yet the one that proved to be most popular, if popularity can be measured by favorable response, was not one that I conceived at all. Although I put it in my own words, the story was told to me by somebody else, and I never considered it to be anything special. The reaction to it made me wonder why I worked so hard to be funny and clever in other columns, many of which never provoked any response at all.

Anyway, in all those years of column writing, I only used a handful of tales such as the one about the bare-bottomed skier, and the rest of this book is made up of my own stuff. These columns might not have proved as popular as the one about the unfortunate skier, but they are, at least, original, and maybe even, I hope, clever and funny.

Life's Little Problems

The Earring in the Underwear

I was laid out in the recliner, watching TV in the dark when my wife Linda came into the room.

She had come from the kitchen where she was washing clothes, and her hand was outstretched as if she were offering something.

I thought she'd brought me a treat. How thoughtful. I reached for it.

She put something into my hand that was small and hard with sharp edges.

"What is it?" I said, smiling.

"It's an earring."

She wasn't smiling.

"An earring?"

I held it up to the light of the TV. An earring, sure enough. The kind that is worn in pierced ears. A small gold heart. Not real gold, just gold colored. Cheap, in other words. The clasp was attached.

"Why are you giving me an earring?" I asked.

"Isn't it yours?" she said.

I thought I detected a chill in her voice.

"Mine?" I said, examining it again. "Not that I know of. I've never owned an earring."

"I found it in your underwear."

"You . . . found . . . an . . . earring . . . in . . . my underwear?" I said, flabbergasted.

"That's what I said."

"It must be yours," I said.

"It's not mine. I've never seen it before. I don't own any earrings like that. "

"I don't know how it got there," I protested, still struck with disbelief. "I think I'd know if I had an earring in my underwear."

"Well, that's where I found it," she said. "I just thought you might want to return it to whoever it belongs to."

"I don't have any idea whose it is," I said. "How can I return it?"

The question was left hanging, because she had turned on her heels and gone back to the laundry. I had the distinct impression that her suspicions were aroused.

But I didn't know what to say or do. After all, how do you explain an earring in your underwear? *Well, see, I was driving down the road and this thing flew in the window and went down my shirt. I thought it was a bug. I tried to get it out, but I couldn't find it. It must've just worked its way down into my underwear.*

No, that would no more fly than an earring would fly in your window.

Must be a practical joke. I'll bet somebody slipped it down the back of my pants when I wasn't looking.

Never wash. Somebody might slip a lizard down your shirt collar but not likely an earring down your pants.

Oh, yeah. I found that. I thought it might be valuable, so I hid it in my underwear. In case somebody tried to rob me, you know, I didn't want them to find it. I just forgot all about it. How much do you think it's worth?

Nope. One glance would tell anybody that thing was worthless.

Is there an ear fairy?

I realized that trying to make an excuse was pointless. Nobody would believe it.

I decided just to say nothing and keep on watching the movie. But few things can distract your attention like the news that an earring has been found in your underwear.

How does something like that happen?

I hadn't done anything to cause an earring to be in my underwear. Honest. And an earring doesn't just jump out of somebody's ear and land in your underwear. Especially with the clasp still attached. I mean, you'd find the ear too in that case, wouldn't you?

Surely nobody would break into your house just to leave an earring in your underwear.

Could I have sat on an earring somewhere that somehow attached to my pants and fell into my underwear when I undressed?

I pondered far into the night without coming up with a satisfactory explanation.

Just another one of those little mysteries of life we all have to live with, I guess.

The Digital Pound

You know how it is some days. You just can't seem to get in step. Things seem to be a beat off. You can't seem to do anything quite right.

I was having a day just like that when I realized I would have to go to the supermarket if I was going to have any supper.

It was bad enough that I forgot to take along the empty bottles for deposit and managed to lose the grocery list on the way, but after I got there I discovered that I don't know anything at all about ordering boiled ham and I'm utterly irresponsible when it comes to parking a cart.

I didn't really intend to order any boiled ham, but I noticed it was on sale as I was passing the deli section, and I'm a sucker for anything on sale.

"I'll have four ounces of that ham sliced thin," I said to the young woman who came to help me from the bakery department, where she'd been negotiating the sale of a Mickey Mouse birthday cake.

"You mean you only want one slice?" she said, looking puzzled.

"No, I don't want it sliced thick," I said, thinking perhaps she had misunderstood me. "I want it sliced thin."

"Still, that won't be but about one slice," she said.

Now it was my turn to look puzzled.

"A quarter of a pound?" I said. "That would have to be a thick slice."

"Oh, you want a quarter of a pound?" she said.

"Yes," I said, relieved that we were now getting on the same wave length.

"Then you want 25 ounces."

"No," I said, again befuddled, "I just want four ounces."

"But that won't be but one slice," she said.

It was clear that we'd reached some sort of impasse, and I wasn't sure how to proceed. Suddenly, her face brightened, as if she'd seen a way out.

She was holding a thick red marking pencil and she placed it on the computerized scale.

"See, that weighs five ounces right there," she said.

"No, that weighs point zero five of a pound," I pointed out. "Five hundredths of a pound."

I was trying to figure out how many ounces that came to but my mind wouldn't calculate that fast.

"A pound is 16 ounces, right?" I said.

"No, a pound is a hundred ounces. See, we have computers now," she said, indicating the digital scale.

"Oh," I said, flabbergasted at what computers had now wrought. "Well, I just want a quarter of a pound."

"So you want 25 ounces."

"I guess so," I said.

"Sliced thin?"

"Sliced thin."

"I see how you're looking at it," she said, attempting to offer me solace as she handed me the ham, but it was clear that she was only feeling sympathy for an old codger that the computer age had left behind with 16-ounce pounds.

I put my 25 ounces of ham in my cart and went away shaking my head in wonder. I got to the produce section before I realized I'd forgotten the peanut butter, which was a couple of aisles back. So I pulled my cart over by the banana bin, left it and went off for the peanut butter.

While I was fetching the Jif, I heard a loud crash from the vicinity of the produce department. I rounded the aisle just in time to see a little old lady, 90 if she was a day, barely tall enough to see over the handle of her grocery cart, whamming into my cart for a second time, sending it reeling against the banana bin.

Worried that my 25 ounces of ham might get bruised, I ran

over and grabbed my cart just as she was backing up for a third run at it.

"Pardon me," I said. "I didn't mean to block the aisle."

"Well, get it out of the way," she snarled, and I did, quickly, watching to see that she didn't take a bead on me.

"You didn't get the toilet paper?" Linda said in exasperation when I got home.

"Just one of those days," I muttered.

Roaches I Have Known

I was having breakfast at a little spot in downtown Chapel Hill recently, reading my favorite newspaper, when I was distracted by sudden movement on the far side of the table.

A cockroach crested the table top and paused, antennae twitching, as if he were considering a run on my sausage and eggs.

"Don't you dare!" I yelped, making a quick swat at him with my napkin.

I missed. He dodged, feinted like a halfback and dashed inside my paper.

I started a frantic search, fanning pages, and found him flattening himself on the editorial page, trying to evade detection next to a Joseph Sobran column, as likely a place as any. When I started to flick him off, he ran for sports. Only then did I realize that this whole newspaper thing was a diversionary tactic.

Another roach had come up on the side of the table and was making a run for my plate, while a third, racing from the same spot as the first, made a shortcut across my whole wheat toast in a bold bid for my hash browns.

I threw down the paper and grabbed to save my plate, smearing my sleeve in egg yolk. (I know you think I'm making this up, but I swear it's the truth.) A brief puzzlement ensued as I held my plate aloft. No roaches underneath.

"Where could they be?" I was asking myself, as I saw one poke his nose over the plate's edge.

I gave up, not so much from loss of appetite, although this certainly was no encouragement to it, as from the realization that this particular breakfast wasn't worth defending. I departed, leaving behind the sports section and a small tip (I figured the roaches would drag it away before the waitress could get to it anyway).

My major regret was that I hadn't put jam on my toast. It might have slowed one of those critters down enough for me to get him, slight satisfaction to be sure for the four bucks I had to pay for the experience, but better than no return at all.

This was not by any means my first experience with roaches in restaurants. I have encountered them in places far fancier. At one posh restaurant, on my first and last visit, I turned up a dead roach in my salad, done in no doubt by vinaigrette poisoning.

I regularly see roaches at my favorite Chinese restaurant, but usually they are on the floor, or on the booth or the wall next to me. But because I like the place otherwise, I just try to ignore them and pretend that they never get into the food or prowl on the dishes or table tops.

One of my most devastating encounters with roaches came last spring, not in a restaurant but a motel. I was in Daytona Beach on a regular trip with a select group of friends to indulge in a bit of masochism at the Jai-Alai matches. Since we always go when college students on spring break have flooded the area (one of our members is a professor who ought to be smarter than to think it possible to win at Jai-Alai), we are not always able to get the best accommodations.

On this trip we were staying in a motel that we had picked out a year earlier. Unbeknownst to us, it had degenerated drastically in that period. We didn't know exactly how drastically until later in the night when we realized that most of the other rooms were occupied by lasciviously clad young women who wandered onto the streets about every half hour and returned with different male companions.

Anyway, on the afternoon that we checked in, we went out to lay in a supply of drinks and munchies. The supermarket we chose had its own bakery with one of the most elaborate displays of luscious delicacies I'd seen in a long time. I, of course, was drawn to it, and after considerable contemplation I chose a lime tart.

This was not just any lime tart, I should point out. This was the most beautiful lime tart I'd ever seen, ornately decorated with creamy white topping, adorned with slivered almonds tinged in a lovely shade of green to match the lime filling. The clerk put it in a fancy box with a cellophane window so that I could see it, and I carried it carefully back to my room, where it was greatly admired by all.

Several times I had to admonish my expeditionary partners to leave that tart alone. Unlike the tarts in nearby rooms, mine was not for sharing. It was to be my treat alone at the conclusion of our night of Jai-Alai.

As it turned out, the thought of that tart was the only thing that pulled me through that sad and miserable night of losing. I couldn't wait to get back to it, and I was filled with delicious expectation when I finally did.

There sat my tart, the box pristine. I picked it up lovingly – and panicked roaches fled from that box in every direction, hordes of roaches, a plague of roaches. They fled onto my hands, up my arms, down my pants legs. Dozens just leapt into space.

I looked down through the cellophane window and saw my beautiful tart marred with little roach trails, like tracks in the snow, and I went into a fury, a regular Mexican hat dance of a fury, toes and heels flailing in every direction.

I must've squashed two dozen of the little buggers, and while I wouldn't exactly call that a victory, considering the loss, it did offer a measure of satisfaction.

Imprisoned Condiments

When the day of the great and final reckoning finally comes, special punishment surely will be reserved for the inventor of those little plastic food packets that are so endearing to restaurants nowadays.

That was a devious soul indeed.

To have conceived these things, no doubt this person must have asked: what can be done to penalize people who want ketchup with their french fries, mayonnaise on their sandwiches, honey on their biscuits or hot sauce on their tacos?

First, I'm sure the thinking went, it should be doled out in miniscule portions. Then it should be encased in such a manner that it is nearly impossible to get at. And if anybody should succeed in the struggle to retrieve it, that person should be made to regret ever wanting it in the first place.

These observations were prompted by a little incident that occurred to me when I stopped in a hurry the other morning and ordered a sausage biscuit with mustard.

"The mustard is behind you," said the person who handed me my biscuit.

I turned to see a tubful of little plastic packets filled with a grayish-yellow substance marked "mustard."

Reluctantly, I picked up a couple and took them with me.

A mistake, of course. It always is a mistake.

One reason is that unless you are Arnold Schwarzenegger, you cannot hope to get inside one of these things with anything of lesser cutting ability than tin snips or an acetylene torch.

The natural reaction, of course, is to go at one of these things with the teeth, which I did. If the incisors are sharp enough, and the jaw strong enough, this works sometimes, and it did in this case. The trouble is that these packets never just open. They erupt.

Mustard, or to be more precise, a facsimile of mustard, dribbled down my chin and plopped onto my shirt. None was left to adorn my sausage.

I managed to wipe most of it off my chin, leaving only a wide faintly yellow smear. Nothing could be done about my shirt, of course. I don't know if a detergent has been made that can deal with mustard stains in fabric. The only recourse once you get mustard on a shirt is to dab mustard all over it and try to do it in a professional enough manner that people will mistake it for polka dots.

I dealt with the second packet a little more adroitly, squeezing a plop onto my sausage. But then I had no way to spread it, except with the flimsy packet, which is not designed for that purpose. I tried it anyway, and ended up spreading it mainly with my fingers.

The two flimsy napkins that I had picked up, already severely taxed by the dribbles on my chin and shirt, were sorely tested in dealing with the necessary cleanup. The result was that I went on my way not only with a yellow shirt but with yellow fingers and a yellow chin.

The most outrageous part of this whole experience, however, was biting into my biscuit and realizing that this yellowish gunk that I had smeared upon my sausage bore not the faintest resemblance to the taste of mustard.

Nothing that comes in these little packets ever tastes like what it is supposed to be. The worst offender of all is this murky liquid that tries to pass as lemon juice. I don't know why so many restaurants find it so difficult to slice actual lemons and serve them with iced tea, but more and more restaurants are passing out these little plastic pouches when lemon is requested.

It may say on the packet that this is lemon juice – although it always adds the disclaimer "reconstituted," whatever that means – but I will never believe it.

It doesn't look like lemon juice, and it most certainly doesn't taste like lemon juice. And if you do manage to get into one of those little packets without all the alleged juice inside running down your hands and into your lap, and if you do get some of it into your tea, you surely will regret it, because your tea suddenly will taste as if it had been made with water from the waste discharge pipes of some chemical company.

When that great day of reckoning does come and the person who conceived these atrocious devices steps forward to receive his just desserts, an appropriate sentence surely would be that in the hereafter he would receive all of his meals in these little packets, and the food inside them would be just as good as the stuff that comes in them now.

Gluteus Minimus

Surely we all have experienced it. That little gleam in the nurse's eye, that touch of glee in her voice when she looks at the doctor's instructions and says, "Oh, we're getting an injection today."

That's not at all what she means, of course. She means that you are getting the injection, or what is better and more commonly described as a "shot." She, or he (for there are many more male nurses nowadays), is going to give it.

And what pleasure they all seem to take from it. Think of the ritual they go through preparing the needle, a needle so long that they have trouble reaching the end of it with their little serum bottles. Can't you just detect their sheer delight when they flash that sadistic little smile and say, "This one's in the hip."

They always call it the hip. All nurses sit on their hips.

So why is it when they give you a shot in the southern reaches of your hip that you can feel it all the way to your shoulder blades? If those needles don't reach that far, they sure seem to.

But let me tell you, friends, you may think you've had it bad in the past when your doctor determined that a shot in the behind was in your best interest, but you don't know the worst of it. More prickly times lie ahead, and you are almost certain to have deeper feelings about this in the future.

I read in the newspaper that a new scientific study has determined that doctors and nurses should start using much longer needles when administering shots in the lower 40, or 48, or whatever your "hip" measurement may be.

The reason for this is that American backsides are growing

broader. Or as the news story so delicately put it, "the padding around the buttocks is so ample on most of us that much of the serum injected gets trapped in the fat and never gets through to the muscle."

The medicine, you see, is supposed to get into muscle tissue in order to distribute it properly through the bloodstream. It is feared that trapping the drug in fat slows its release and delays or alters its effects.

But those needles that look and feel so long are actually so short that they don't penetrate "the fat pads covering the gluteus maximus muscles," as the study put it, on most Americans. The study ascertained that the medicine is getting through to muscle in less than 15 percent of men who get shots in the area under discussion. The figure is less than 6 percent in women.

This disparity is due to women having more natural padding on their bottoms than men, an average of 2.5 centimeters, regardless of weight, although in my experience this has seemed, like the size of needles, much greater (but I will mention no names).

What bothers me particularly about all this is that those of us who are in arrears, so to speak, in gaining bottom padding are going be the butt of undue punishment because this. Why should we have to face . . . well, back up to needles capable of being used in fencing matches just because everybody else is growing broader in the beam?

It's unfair, and those of us afflicted with this minority condition – gluteus minimus it might be called – ought to get behind a movement to do something about it. I don't know what we could call it, maybe Little Needles for Little Buns, but the point is, in our cases, this whole matter of needles has already gone entirely too far.

Digging the Root Canal

I knew from the moment I bit into the pizza slice and my head snapped upright with pain; knew it in my very marrow.

The verdict was inevitable, dreaded though it was, and I shuddered upon hearing the words.

Root canal.

With all the advances in modern dentistry you'd think that somebody would have come up with a more pleasant name for this particular bit of dental wizardry.

Root canal sounds harsh and blunt, and it doesn't exactly conjure up pleasant images.

Actually, dentists do have another, more sophisticated name for root canal – endodontic therapy. But they must have trouble pronouncing it, because you never hear a dentist say, "I need to perform a little endodontic therapy on that tooth."

No, they throw "root canal" right at you, and while your poor tooth is quivering and you're still shuddering, they even begin to describe exactly how they will ream that sucker out and nail it down. No pretty words to ease the way, just blatant drilling and digging and pounding, with pulp flying in all directions.

In my case, a root canal was just the beginning of my agonies. The troublesome tooth was one that would have to anchor a long-needed bridge. To build this bridge, two other teeth would have to be ground down, one to be almost totally reconstructed.

Postponing all this work any further would just make things worse and more difficult, the dentist was telling me, as my mind searched frantically for reasons to put it off.

He was ready to start on the root canal right then, and the

only response I could come up with that would provide immediate escape and delay was a decision to have all the work done at once.

That would require three hours in the chair, my dentist said, looking a little skeptical (he knows me, after all, and was probably concerned about having the rescue squad standing by) but I readily agreed for immediate reprieve.

Two weeks. That was how long it took to fit in the appointment, how long I had to let those three excruciating hours grow into torturous months in my mind, to let that root canal become the digging of the Panama, the grinding of those anchor teeth the strip mining of mountains.

A Sony Walkman is the answer, several people told me when, seeking sympathy, I foisted my dread onto them. Just put those earphones on, tune into some rock and roll and let the dentist do what he must. Not only will the music drown out the terrible sound of the drilling, but you can lose yourself in it and forget the indignities taking place in your mouth.

It sounds like a good theory, but I'm here to tell you that it doesn't work. That drilling is already inside your head, not outside forcing its way in. The drilling and the music just assault your brain from different directions, setting up a cacophony that is truly mind-scrambling.

The amazing thing to me after trying this theory is that some people actually put on those headphones and pump that music directly into their heads without being in a dentist's chair. The long-term effect surely must do to the brain what a root canal does to a tooth.

The sad truth is that when you are undergoing such heavy dental construction as bridge building and canal digging, nothing, not even the pain of force-fed rock-and-roll, can cause you to ignore what is going on in your mouth.

At one point, while the bulldozers were revving up and the foundation-drilling rig was being moved in, an inner tube from a tractor tire was stretched over the inside of my mouth for some reason – to prevent erosion during the canal job, I suspect – and fastened with an elaborate set of clamps. It's hard to ignore.

Another time, I opened my eyes just in time to see a crane lifting a horseshoe-shaped steel plate into place in the bottom of my mouth. That was just before the cement mixer backed up and dumped in a load, as I recall, the first of several, and every time that cement began to set it was pried out with crowbars.

Like all construction work, this took a little longer than anticipated, and it isn't over yet. Only a temporary bridge is now installed; the permanent one is still to be erected.

And after that comes something even more agonizing and excruciating than what I've already endured: paying the bill. If I'm able to get the money together, my dentist ought to be able to buy himself another bulldozer.

From Cockamamie to Cock-a-leekie

I realize this whole thing may sound a little cockamamie, but it shows how easy it is to get distracted and carried away.

Cockamamie, in fact, is how it got started. I wanted to use the word in a column. I'd heard it all my life. I knew what it meant – silly or nonsensical – but I wasn't sure how to spell it.

Following my policy of always seeking the easy way out if possible, I asked several people seated near me in the newsroom. Nobody knew how to spell it, of course, so I got up and trudged to the fat *Webster's Third New International Dictionary*, Unabridged, which I still have trouble lifting even after a year of Nautilus training.

The problem inherent in using a dictionary to spell a word is, of course, that you have to know how to spell it to look it up. You sort of have to feel, or more aptly, sound your way along.

Cock-a-mamie, I said to myself. So I turned to the c's and went straight for cocka.

Cock-a-doodle-doo was there. So was cock-and-bull and a whole lot more of which I'd never heard. But I didn't spot cockamamie.

Maybe it's cockermamie, I thought.

Cockermeg was there – temporary supports in a coal mine. I'd never heard of that. Never heard of cockernony either. That's the gathering of a young woman's hair under a snood.

A snood?

What in the world is a snood? I turned to the s's. A snood, it turns out is a net for holding the back of a young woman's hair, usually attached to a hat, although it also can be the fleshy protuberance at the base of a turkey's bill.

I started to look up turkey to see if there was a picture of one so I'd know what its snood looked like when it struck me that I was trying to spell cockamamie.

Back to the c's.

Could it be cochamamie?

Cochliomyia, I found – anything spiral – before I got completely wrapped up in cochineal, which is a red dye made from the dried bodies of female cochineal insects.

Cochineal insects are common in Central and South America. They are red and look like mealy bugs and feed mainly on cochineal figs which aren't figs but cactuses. Farmers cultivate cochineal figs so they can attract and catch cochineal insects and sell them to make dye. The dye comes out different colors depending on which species of bugs you boil and how you boil them. It once was used a lot for wool and food coloring but is primarily a biological marker nowadays.

After that fascinating interlude, I had to think a minute to remember what it was I was trying to look up.

Oh, yeah, cockamamie. Was there any other way it could be spelled? Surely I just overlooked it back among the cockas. It's too common a word not to be there.

Cock-a-maroo was the closest thing to it. That's Russian bagatelle, which, I discovered by turning back to the b's, is either a trifle, a short piece of music or a billiards-like game.

Cock-a-hoop, I noticed, back again in the c's. It means elated or triumphantly boastful. Cock-a-whoop, too. That's heralding speech.

I learned that the difference between a cockatiel and a cockatoo, both crested parrots, is primarily size, cockatoos being larger. I also learned that a cockatoo bush and a cockatoo fence have nothing to do with cockatoos. One is a blueberry bush, the other a rough fence made of logs or saplings.

A cockarouse, I was fascinated to find, was a person of consequence among American colonists. A cockarouse might also have been a cockatrice, which is either an extremely offensive person or a legendary creature with the head, wings and legs of a cock and the tail of a serpent.

A cockapert cockalorum could also indulge in cockalorum, although not likely with a cockatouche. Maybe with a cockawee, though.

Cockapert is impudent, while cockalorum is either a strutting little fellow or a game of leapfrog. A cockatouche is a tiny fish that lives deep in the Great Lakes. A cockawee is an old squaw.

Cock-a-leekie wasn't at all what I imagined it might be. It's chicken soup with leeks. While we're on comestibles, ever hear of cock ale? It's a brew made of fermented fruits, spices and the mincemeat of a boiled male fowl. That should be cause for giving up drinking.

I was getting an education but I wasn't any closer to learning how to spell cockamamie. I went in search of other dictionaries.

In the library I found three more fat ones, including one devoted to slang, but no cockamamie in any.

Well, if it's not in the dictionary, I can spell it any way I want to, I'd decided, when my friend Stan Swofford found it in his paperback copy of *The New York Times Everyday Dictionary*.

Cockamamie or cockamamy, it said to my great relief. At least I didn't have to risk going off half-cocked.

Seeing Double

It took a while for me to realize what was wrong. I was driving to work when it happened. Suddenly, I started feeling strange. I kept blinking and rubbing my eyes, thinking it might go away. It didn't.

By the time I got to work, I knew the problem. I was seeing double. Not all the time. It would come and go. But it was coming and going with increasing frequency.

I was complaining about it with friends at lunch.

"I think I'm going to have to see a doctor," I said.

"I guess you'll see two, won't you?" said Stan Swofford.

"At least you won't have any trouble getting a second opinion," said Jack Scism.

It never pays to complain about medical problems at lunch.

By mid-afternoon and mid-column, my double vision seemed to have come to stay. On my computer screen, I was seeing two lines for every one I wrote, one slightly above the other, like a ghost image on TV. And despite quips that this way I'd only have to write half as much, I was getting worried.

I tried to call my doctor but discovered he was on vacation. I tried another doctor of my acquaintance. He was out of town. Friends in the newsroom finally urged me to call their ophthalmologist. Better come right out, I was told.

After a thorough examination, the doctor returned to tell me the problem was not in my eyes. My vision was fine. But the muscles that control my left eye were failing, causing my eyes to move out of sync. He thought that I should see a neurologist. Immediately. He'd arrange the appointment.

I drove to the neurologist's office with increasing anxiety.

After filling out forms, I was given a checklist with scores of maladies and conditions. I had few checks. Except for a touch of hypochondria (well, maybe more than a touch), an ulcer long ago and an occasional bout of the flu I've never been sick. I've never been in a hospital, never missed a work day because of illness.

Ushered into an examination room, I waited with *People* magazine, seeing two of Victoria Principal, the first advantage of my condition. The doctor came in, asked a lot of questions, told me to strip to my underwear and left. He returned to poke, prod, prick, knock and tickle, checking parts that I never before had considered to have even the remotest connection to my eyes.

The diagnosis: fourth cranial nerve palsy. Sometimes it comes upon people with no explainable reason, the doctor said, then goes away on its on. Sometimes the reasons are explainable. One of them is brain tumor.

When a doctor mentions brain tumor and it is .your brain that he is talking about, it tends to rivet your attention.

He'd seen no signs that I had a tumor, he said. Other problems could be the cause. In all probability, the cause would not be found and the condition would go away, maybe in a few days, maybe six weeks, maybe six months. But he wanted to do additional tests, scans of the brain, visual and auditory evoked responses.

I left the office in a daze, my brain searching frantically for an intruder in its midsts. By the time I got back to the newsroom and my unfinished column, well past deadline, I could feel the tumor actually growing in my brain. I had started off to work that day feeling fine and now I was trying to finish a column while planning final farewell speeches to family and friends.

I slept little that night, and when I did sleep, I was disturbed by dreams even more weird than usual, surely tumor-induced, I figured. At 6:45 next morning, an hour that normally finds me snoozing, I was on my way to Greensboro to be introduced to the so-called CAT Scan machine.

I was given a flowery shower cap to don and placed supine

on a mechanized stretcher with the instruction that I had to hold my head perfectly still, lest I have to do the whole thing over again. For the next 40 minutes, during half of which brain dye was gurgling into my veins, my head moved in and out of the doughnut like a finger tip prodding the hole. The machine whirred and whined at many decibels, and inside the hole, a band of light in varying shades of gray whirled periodically. I couldn't figure whether I felt as if I were playing a part in a science-fiction movie or testing a new ride at Carowinds.

"Everything looks fine," the doctor said, after I delivered the scan results to his office.

No tumor! I felt like dancing and waltzed off to a little room with him to look at the pictures of my brain, an opportunity I couldn't resist. How many people, after all, get the chance to see proof that they have brains? Despite what you may have read in letters to the editor, mine, I'm happy to report, is larger than a pea.

We'd know more after the other tests three days hence, the doctor said. Meanwhile, I could stop the double vision by wearing a patch. I showed up at the office looking as rakish as the Hathaway shirt man only to be hailed as "Ahoy, matey," and Moshe Dayan.

For the evoked responses tests, sensors were attached to my scalp and the backs of my ear lobes and hooked to a computer where I could watch my brain draw pictures of mountain ranges with purple lines of majesty. For the first tests, I was instructed to stare at a red dot in the center of a TV screen while a pattern of black and white squares flashed back and forth in what appeared to be a kaleidoscope of patterns.

"Hey, this is just like Mr. Peanut," I said to the technician, who gave me a befuddled look.

I went on to explain that when I was a kid, Planter's peanuts came with little cards bearing a picture of Mr. Peanut with a red dot in his belly and instructions to stare at the dot, then look at the sky. When you did, you'd see Mr. Peanut in the sky.

I don't think the young technician, reared on the wonders of computers, could properly appreciate the magic of Mr.

Peanut in the sky. I'm not sure she even knew who Mr. Peanut is. The second hour of my tests was devoted to listening to constant clicking through headphones.

No abnormalities, the doctor said. My double vision, which already was clearing, was unexplainable and no doubt would go away of its own volition.

But surely there had to be *some* reason for it, I pressed.

Well, yes, the doctor said, but there was only one sure way of finding it – autopsy.

"Think I'll pass," I said.

It wasn't until I left his office that I realized I had this clicking in my ears.

Just Trying To Be Helpful

Roach Sex on Capitol Hill

Just when we begin thinking that Washington has come up with every possible cockamamie scheme (in this case maybe cockaroachamamie would be a better description) for spending our money something always comes along to show us how wrong we can be.

Consider this little story that hit the wires recently. Seems there is a terrible cockroach infestation in congressional offices on Capitol Hill, which isn't surprising when you think about it, considering the sleazy environment cockroaches prefer.

So what does Congress do about it? Do they call Otto the Orkin Man or set out cheap little Roach Motels like the rest of us?

Of course not.

They opt for cockroach sex palaces.

Listen to how these new "rectangular plastic traps" work. They emit synthesized male sexual scents of seven cockroach species. This lures female roaches into the black boxes "where they are zapped with a small electrical charge."

Stunned, the females fall into a glue pit and become trapped. "The females then emit their own sexual scent," the story went on. "That draws ardent male cockroaches."

Cockroaches must be really different from most creatures. If I'd just been zapped by an electrical charge and dumped flailing and kicking into a glue pit, emitting sexual scents probably would be the last thing on my mind.

Anyway, the males come in looking for the stuck females and end up themselves in the glue pit (didn't Mama warn you about the pits of depravation where sex could lead you?).

There all are supposed to die eventually of starvation, if not from excessive scent emissions.

If this seems an overly elaborate and less than sporting way to deal with a cockroach problem, look at another aspect of it – cost – and that should easily overshadow any other considerations you may have about the situation.

Each of these little roach sex palaces costs $359. I've done some figuring, and if just one trap is put in each congressional office, that will come to an initial outlay of $192,065. I say initial outlay, because each trap requires another $162 worth of accessories annually at an overall cost of $86,670.

When they say accessories, I'm sure they don't mean little roach waterbeds and hot tubs. From the description offered, I can only conclude that means fresh glue for the glue pits.

Eighty-six thousand dollars worth of glue? That ought to be a lot of glue. Unless it's ordered by the Pentagon. In that case it probably would be just a little tube barely big enough to put a model airplane together, hardly enough to deal with even a single one of the bloated cockroaches that surely must prowl the halls of Congress.

These expenditures, however, are no doubt just the beginning of cost. Somebody will have to go around and pick all those cockroaches out of those little boxes and change the glue, which no doubt will dry quickly. I'm sure the honorables themselves aren't going to do this.

No telling how many new federal employees with overly generous benefits will be required for the job, or what that additional expense might be.

It would be interesting to have a study done on these roach traps to see how many roaches they catch and exactly what the cost per roach comes to.

Seems to me it might be a lot cheaper just to set a bounty on Capitol Hill roaches – say 10-cents a roach – and let any members of Congress or their staffs who need extra spending money go stomping after the devious little creatures.

Come to think of it, if Congress spent more time chasing roaches and less thinking up inventive ways to waste our money, we'd probably all be better off.

The Official Tongue

Thankfully, we don't have to go all the way to Washington to find truly inane political antics. Our own state legislature, I notice, forges bravely on, tackling one serious problem after another.

Not too long ago, it acted on an issue that surely will soon concern us all. It made English the official language of North Carolina.

What worries me about that is this: When do we have to start speaking it?

And what if we don't get it right?

I mean, I flunked English in high school, and I had trouble getting through it in summer school. Does this mean I'll have to go back to Mrs. Modlin's class until I pass with something more than a U (we were graded with Ex, S, U, and F – excellent, satisfactory, unsatisfactory and fail)? If I can't bring it up to an S, will I be subject to being expelled from the state?

Will the state soon be creating patrols of language police to make sure we are living up to the legislature's expectations?

If they do, won't a healthy portion of the people now occupying the eastern half of this state end up in prison?

And what about Wilson (Woolson to those who live there), where the people speak a language so peculiar that it only faintly resembles the mother tongue? That place no doubt will be a ghost town if this law is enforced.

The trouble with this law, as I see it, was summed up by Rep. Mickey Michaux of Durham during the debate in the House, when he questioned what would be considered proper English.

"If you ask people from England, who speak English,

whether or not Americans speak English, the answer is an emphatic no," he said. Just what is acceptable English and who's going to decide? The legislature didn't bother to get into that. It has adopted an official language for us without telling us what it really is. And in a state with such a hodge-podge of regional dialects that is certain to create a lot of concern and confusion.

What about all of those Outer Bankers who still say "hoigh toide" for high tide? Will they be able to keep doing that? Some people say they are merely speaking remnants of old English, or is it olde English? Is old English better than new English, or vice versa? Just who's going to work up the courage to approach some independent and cantankerous mountaineer who insists on saying "hit" for "it" and tell him that he can't speak hillbilly anymore? It surely won't be some legislator from Down East, because neither would be able to understand a word the other was saying.

And what about this slopover effect?

I'm talking about all the people along the northern fringes of this state who talk that funny Virginia language, always saying "aboot" for "about" and other weird things. And all those people, primarily down along the southeastern edges of the state, who've been influenced by South Carolinese. Heaven only knows what they're saying.

Will this be tolerated now?

That brings up another question. What about all those outsiders who've been flocking to North Carolina in recent years? You know who I mean. Yankees. Has anybody yet been able to figure out what they're talking about? Are they going to have to start talking like the rest of us if they want to stay? Which ones of us are they going to have to start talking like? It's only fair to tell them.

Somebody ought to be pressing the legislature to tell us just which brand of English we've adopted and what kind of time frame we're going to have in which to learn it. Right now everything is awfully vague.

The senator who introduced this legislation, one Frank Block, who hails from that hotbed of linguistic purity, New

Hanover County, says that its purpose is to "preserve, protect and strengthen the English language."

"It gets to the policy of the state," he said. "It sets a direction that in the future it will be well known that English is the official language and that is the language which the state (uses) to conduct public policy."

I'm not sure exactly what that means, but it may mean that only people who conduct the state's business are going to have to worry about this law. In that case, it could prove to be a good thing.

Imagine if educators and bureaucrats and lawyers suddenly had to abandon the gobbledygook they hold so dear and start writing and speaking in plain English.

It's a concept too bold to grasp, a spectacle too breathtaking to behold.

Why, if through some miracle it should happen, it might even lead legislators to begin enacting laws that make sense enough for all of us to understand.

Lawyers R Us

If we ever did enforce a law that requires all residents of North Carolina to speak English, the lawyers would be the first ones kicked out of the state, which may be reason enough to enforce such a law.

I never really understood why lawyers can't seem to speak so that the rest of us can understand them. They are all supposedly intelligent folks, with years of college and law school. You would think that sometime during all those years of schooling somebody would have taught them to speak clearly, but obviously no one did.

What I want to know is if lawyers are so smart, why do they give their law firms such dreadfully long and boring names?

You know what I mean. Bilgewater, Blowhard, Loophole, Hokum & Sludge. Just to name a short one.

Every law firm in the country seems to be named by stringing out the last names of the senior partners.

I'm not sure whether this indicates a lack of imagination or an ego problem. Probably both.

Maybe it's just that lawyers want to appear stodgy and stuffy and overblown. I don't know. Certainly a long string of difficult names is intimidating, and lawyers appear to enjoy few things more than intimidating people.

Of course, there comes a point where even lawyers have to stop. These firms that employ scores, even hundreds, of lawyers can't possibly string all their names together. There wouldn't be room on the office door. And their letterheads would consume all of their stationery, leaving no space to write threatening or obfuscatory letters. They'd be so bogged down by their names that they would be put out of business.

Which may not be such a bad idea now that I think about it.

But consider the poor secretaries who have to answer the phones. If law firms didn't restrict those tangles of names at some point, the secretaries would be half a day trying to answer a single call. It's hard enough on law firm secretaries who only have to try to wrap their tongues around a half dozen or so convoluted names every time the phone rings.

I always wonder if they're reading them anyway. "Good morning, Windbag, Finagler, Gougeham, Sleazebaugh, Flatulence and Bunkum. Can I help you?" I mean, I can't imagine anybody remembering all of those names in proper sequence and repeating them dozens of times a day.

That's the trouble with law firm names. Nobody can remember them.

The only law firm name that I can remember is the one from the old joke: Dewey, Cheatham & Howe. All others are just a jumble.

It's almost impossible to look up a law firm in the telephone book without turning to the yellow pages and wading through all the listings hoping to spot a recognizable name. The names in law firm titles are almost never in alphabetical order, and there seem to be no discernible patterns in how they are strung together. More often than not, they aren't even rhythmical. If they were, that might help a little in remembering them.

It makes you wonder how the order of these names is decided. Do they put all of them into a hat and draw? Do they flip coins or arm wrestle? Or do they just sit down and try every possible combination until they come up with the one that is most difficult to roll off the tongue and remember?

Another question: How do they decide whether or not to use commas to separate the names? Some do, some don't. Then comes the ampersand problem. Most seem to prefer it but a few stick in "and."

As traditional as they may seem, law firm names have no obvious order at all. They are a confusion, which shouldn't be surprising, considering that they are put together by lawyers.

Clearly, though, time has come for law firms to move into

the new age and begin giving themselves catchier names, as many stodgy old corporations already have done. Something short and punchy. Something that will define the work in which the firms specialize so that people don't have to listen to secretaries spouting hundreds of names before they find a law firm that can handle their cases. Something, in short, that somebody can remember.

For example, law firms that deal primarily in criminal cases might call themselves Not Guilty, or Sprung!, or Off Easy, although the latter might cause some problems from those oven-cleaning people (which surely would gladden the hearts of their lawyers).

A law firm aiming for personal injury cases could call itself No Pain, No Gain.

Surely Legal Weasels would be an apt handle for a firm that sends lawyers to hang around courthouses waiting for widows' houses to be put up at tax sales.

And how about BULL for a Wall Street firm? Wouldn't a law firm that sought to represent defense contractors have a real advantage if it called itself Overruns R Us?

I don't expect any sudden changes, of course, but I always strive to be helpful. Even to lawyers.

Charlotte: The Modest City

Rolfe Neill is an acquaintance of mine who also always strives to be helpful. An honest man with a good tan, Rolfe, publisher of the *Charlotte Observer*, a fair-to-middling newspaper, is naturally opposed to bluster.

A couple of years back he presided over the dropping of *The Observer*'s long-time slogan, "Foremost Newspaper of the Carolinas," which he called an "embarrassing bit of puffery." Now he is going after the boosters who keep touting Charlotte as a "world-class city."

"Ugh," Rolfe says of that description.

The problem with calling Charlotte a world-class city, Rolfe says, is that it just ain't so. And a new coliseum, a direct flight to London and new NBA team (he failed to mention the world's longest stock car race) don't make it so.

No sense in pretending, says Rolfe. For Charlotte ever to be considered as a world-class city, which he thinks improbable, several hundred years must elapse. Charlotte, he thinks, should aspire to something more realistic.

Such as "a city of excellence."

But even that, Rolfe notes, is a long way off, for when it comes to such things as education, parks, geographical features, arts, universities, research facilities, libraries and restaurants, just to name a few things (for some reason he left out newspapers), Charlotte can't yet make such a claim.

"When aspiring to excellence," he wrote, "we must look at the decades, not the clock. Nobody ever earned excellence on the quick. The reason it's rare is that excellence requires not only hard work but sustained commitment, a dedication of which few are capable."

This is all well and good, if not excellent, and Rolfe certainly is to be commended for his honesty and his campaign against bloated boasting. But until future decades have had a chance to prove whether Charlotte can achieve excellence, if not world-class, Charlotte is left without a slogan. Clearly, no city with any pride wants to find itself in such a deprived and embarrassed state. And Rolfe offers no substitutions at all.

Fortunately for Charlotte, I like the place, lacking though it may be, and as a favor to the city where I once was employed by Rolfe's newspaper, I want to do something for it. So in keeping with Rolfe's ideas of straightforward and honest claims, I have come up with a few slogans that Charlotte might use until it can do better.

My proposals:
- Charlotte: the So-So City
- Charlotte: a City Not Much Different from Any Other, Everything Considered
- Charlotte: a City of Tall Buildings and Short Success
- Charlotte: an OK Place for Not-Too-Picky People
- Charlotte: a Low-Class, or Maybe Even No-Class City
- Charlotte: a City of a Few Fairly Good Things, a Lot More That's Mediocre and Some Plain Bad Stuff
- Charlotte: Where Mundane Must Do Until Urbane Sets In
- Charlotte: Low on Accomplishment But High on Hope
- Charlotte: a City Where Some of the Women Ain't Too Fat But a Lot Are
- Charlotte: a Southern City with No Barbecue Fit to Mention
- Charlotte: a City That Tries Now and Then but Not too Hard
- Charlotte: a City That Never Quite Lives Up
- Charlotte: a City of Little But Exceptionally Bad Sculpture
- Charlotte: the Queen City (But Not the Kind You're Probably Thinking)
- Charlotte: a Pedestrian City Whose Streets Ain't Made for Walkin' (Except by a Few Accommodating Citizens in

Very Tight, Very Short Skirts and High White Boots.
- Charlotte: an All Right Kind of Place if You Don't Expect Much
- Charlotte: Where Indifference Matters
- Charlotte: A World-Class City Only in the Sense That It Happens to Be On the World But Then So Is Newark
- Charlotte: Home of Jim and Tammy and a Good Many Other Sleazy People
- Charlotte: Who Cares?

Surely Charlotte can find one of these that will be suitable. I offer them free of charge. No need for credit.

Who Doesn't Run Greensboro

A while ago the *Greensboro News & Record* decided to tout its home city. Editors rushed through the newsroom shouting orders to various reporters.

A friend of mine was given the choice assignment of uncovering who really runs Greensboro and the Triad, finding the movers and the shakers. I was hoping that I had been spared from participating and was slowly making my way toward the door in case I hadn't, when I heard my editor's gruff voice call out "Where's Bledsoe?"

My assignment, he told me was to compile a list of the least influential people in Greensboro. I would prefer to think that the assignments were distributed randomly and that it was just chance that I was chosen for this one.

Before we get on to this less-than-eagerly awaited list, however, let me first offer a few words about methodology.

Just how did I go about determining who should be on this list?

Well, I began by combining three basic methods used by academic researchers. In large part, I relied on the "disreputational" approach – a two-step (backward) investigation of who is known for never getting anything done.

I also focused on issues to see who had so little concern for them that they had difficulty deciding which ones to ignore. Academic researchers call this the "indecisional" approach.

In addition, I searched bars, alleys, editorial offices and bus station rest rooms to see who sits around most of the time doing nothing. Academic researchers call this the "posteriorial" approach.

Finally, I made up a list of 143,000 people who might

qualify for the list and submitted it to a panel of confirmed ne'er-do-wells who asked themselves a series of questions, none of which they bothered to answer.

After becoming utterly confused by an elaborate numbering system, the panel sifted and winnowed until several passed out from over-exertion. Revived and spurred by a promise of free drinks, the panel at last produced a list of 30 bottom vote getters that was put into a mayonnaise jar and submitted to a tarot card reader to determine if the list might contain any "concealed" or "symbolic" failures. The jar was tossed into Buffalo Creek and forgotten.

I then made up the list of the least influential people in Greensboro off the top of my head.

I offer it herewith. The order of presentation, I should add, is not necessarily indicative of anything.

• Tay Won On, martial arts instructor to city councilman Bill Burckley. "Always remember," Tay told Burckley, "lesson number one, the Master says, 'Never dump Bloody Mary on head of anybody twice your size.' "

• Joe Fryem Brittle, assistant district attorney who counseled his boss, Jim Kimel, "Whatever we do, we've got to go for the death penalty on this Coulthard case. If he doesn't get it, nobody should."

• Ever Bigger Debbits, public relations consultant to Roger Soles, president of Jefferson-Pilot. "What you need to do, Roger, is to open up a little and show people your warm side. Talk to the press. And don't forget to smile when the photographer shows up."

• Dewey Hairpeace, meteorological consultant. "What people want in their weather reports," Hairpeace advised Channel 2's Randy Jackson, "is a sophisticated, scientific approach. Some goofballs try the good-ol'-boy route, broadcasting from their back yards, wearing baseball caps that viewers send in and even going to their houses for dinner, if you can believe it. You'll never get anywhere doing that."

• Cauccious Dollars, financial adviser to chiropractor Russell Cobb. "Move slowly," Dollars cautioned his client. "Don't borrow unless it's necessary. Never overextend. Don't let ego lead you to take on more than you can handle."

• High Feeze, attorney for former coliseum manager Jim Oshust. "If you get called as a witness in that coliseum embezzlement trial, Jim," Feeze counseled his client, "don't say a thing. Take the Fifth."

• George Trot, poll taker for slow runners and campaign adviser to Tom Gilmore: "Forget this race, Tom," Trot said. "Nobody with Groucho Marx eyebrows has ever been elected to Congress."

• Madame Fastrack, Jaycee palmist and personality consultant to Jim Melvin. "No wonder people think you're bland, Jim," Madame Fastrack is reported to have told the most powerful man in Greensboro. "Just look at you. Get rid of that brown suit. Lighten up. Wear a Harley Davidson t-shirt to your next board meeting. Try a punk hair-do. Learn to Moon Walk. Conduct your next business session in rap."

The Greenhouse Effect

I don't know about you, but I am getting more than a little frightened about what has been happening with the weather.

Just look at all of those long stretches of nearly unbearable heat that we had to endure this summer.

The very earth was scorched. Creeks dried up. Reservoirs emptied and cracked. Trees turned brown and died. Stunted crops withered in the fields. Poultry expired in ranks. Dogs stumbled around panting with their tongues hanging out. People huddled in air-conditioned refuges – at least those who could did.

And this may be just a taste of what is to come, we are told. The world is heating up. Weather patterns are changing, and the whole face of Earth may be altered by it.

The polar ice caps may melt, raising the levels of the oceans and washing over low-lying areas such as New York City and the whole state of Florida. Previously lush areas such as North Carolina could turn into deserts. Our mountains could erode into the sea, which might be lapping somewhere around Siler City.

The reason for all of this, I keep reading and hearing, is this ominous "greenhouse effect." Almost daily we are treated to more dire predictions about this thing. "Greenhouse is unstoppable, scientists warn," read a front-page headline.

Excuse me, but I just can't understand why this has been allowed to develop into such a problem. Why are greenhouse owners allowing all of this heat to escape in the first place? Are they just leaving the doors wide open? Or are greenhouses just so poorly insulated that owners are powerless to stop them from releasing so much heat and messing everything up?

Perhaps the bigger question is this: Why do we have to have so many greenhouses anyway?

I mean, what do we get from greenhouses? Potted plants and hanging baskets, right? Stuff to keep inside slowly dying. Are we really willing to sacrifice all that grows outside so that we can huddle inside, air-conditioned, watering anemic plants? Are we really willing to risk our food supply so that patrons can fight their way through ferns in yuppie restaurants?

It seems apparent that we'd better start doing something about all these greenhouses before it's too late.

While I am on the weather, let me take up a few other matters that have been bothering me lately. These "meteorologists" on TV, for one. Not so many years ago, most TV stations had very attractive young women who told us about the weather. They were called "weather girls," and they always smiled prettily when they told about tornadoes ravaging trailer parks in Alabama or Oklahoma.

Now we have only "meteorologists" or people certified by various meteorological societies, and there is not a pretty young female among them. They are all earnest young men who hunker constantly over radar screens and computer keyboards when they are not telling us how highly trained they are or showing us their colorful and ever-moving charts. They are supported by huge banks of highly sophisticated equipment which always loom in the background as they talk.

But despite all of this, the weather has not improved one whit since these guys came along. Indeed, it has grown demonstrably worse, and I'm not sure that greenhouses can be blamed for all of it.

Let me ask you this. Before these guys came along, had you ever heard of the "heat index"? Now, every time it gets insufferably hot, they drag this thing out to make it even hotter than it actually is. Who do they think they are anyhow?

Another thing about these guys: why can they never let it hail without telling us what size the hailstones are? Usually, they are marble-size. Sometimes they are even golf-ball-size. Once in a while they are pea-size. I have never heard of BB-size hail, but I did once hear of some that supposedly was baseball-size, although I suspect that actually was just some meteorologist's fondest fantasy.

I'm sure that the first day in meteorology school these guys are given a kit containing a dried pea, a marble, a golf ball, maybe a tennis ball and a baseball and told to keep it handy so they can always be prepared to rush out and measure any hail that falls (although they never allow it just to fall; it always pelts or batters).

Not long ago, one of these guys must have been caught without his kit, because I heard him describe some hail as dime-size. Obviously, he used the only thing he had at hand to measure the stuff without realizing the limitations of a dime for such duty. Either that or thin, flat hail fell for the first time in history.

Well, thank you for letting me get all of this off my mind. I feel a lot cooler now.

When You Have to G-G-Go

Those Greensboro Jaycees, clever fellows, rarely miss a trick. But no matter how you feel about the Jaycees, you have to admit that one of their new schemes almost touches bottom.

The Jaycees have developed an advertising concept that's sure to command attention. You might even say it'll provide a locked-in audience.

The Jaycees are selling ads to be posted inside the portable toilets, formally called Porta-Johns, at the Greater Greensboro Open golf tournament.

That's right, friends, for only $30, you or your company can sponsor one of the 100 Porta-Johns that will be placed around the Forest Oaks Country Club golf course during the GGO.

"It's something brand new," says Weldon Gann, the car salesman who came up with the idea. He's "sanitation engineer" for this year's GGO. That means he's in charge of renting the Porta-Johns, placing them strategically and keeping them emptied and cleaned. It's a thankless job. No wonder he dreams of greater glories.

"I know it sounds a little tacky," Gann says of his concept, "but I think it's time it got started. It's something to have some fun with. You could put your boss's picture in there. You can say anything you want. Of course, we don't want any profanity or anything in bad taste."

Clearly, Gann is a man of vision. I don't know why this idea hasn't already caught on big. After all, what do you do when you go into a public toilet? You read the graffiti right? (Unless you're the base sort who scrawls the stuff.) It's a natural spot for advertising.

Gann expected quick responses from letters offering the ads he recently sent to all GGO sponsors and Jaycees. Those letters even offered some ready-made ads to choose from:

Toi-let You Know, We Support The GGO . . .

A-commode-ating You And The GGO . . .

We're Helping Anyway We Can.

So far, Gann reports, the response has not been especially moving. A few people, mostly other Jaycees, have told him they will buy ads. One fellow called to inquire about putting Sheriff Paul Gibson's picture in one of the units, and the Guilford Republican Executive Committee jokingly endorsed a resolution to have "Vote Democrat" plastered across some of the Porta-John seats.

Apparently, a lot of people are laughing, but few are putting up money. Gann isn't discouraged. "We're just getting started," he says. Indeed, the Jaycees plan to begin a telephone campaign soon to sell the ads.

I would never presume to tell the Jaycees how to go about their business, but it seems to me that if they don't want to get caught with their pants down on this thing and flush away any hope for success, they're going to have to line up the proper advertisers for the medium.

This requires some careful and creative thought and I have devoted what little I could muster to the problem in recent days. Consequently, I've come up with a few ads I'm sure the Jaycces could sell if they tried, and they are welcome to use them as my little contribution to the success of the GGO.

See what you think of these:

• *While you are reading this, you may be destroying your shine. Restore and protect it with Griffin's Water-Proof Shoe Polish.*

• *Sitting there all broken-hearted, needing to go and can't get started? Sure starts every time with Sears' Die-Hard batteries.*

I'm convinced that the Jaycees could greatly increase their chances of sales if they also offered ads on the outsides of the Porta-Johns.

It might even be a good place for a newspaper ad, considering that so many newspapers are read in toilets anyway.

How about:

When you have to G-G-Go at the GGO, take along a G-G-Good newspaper, the G-G-Greensboro Daily News.

And this would seem to be a sure-fire prospect:

Thanks for enjoying our products, but please don't allow them to disturb the golfers. This silencer cubicle provided by Luck's Beans.

But maybe the Jaycees, as image-conscious as they've been lately, are saving the outsides of the Porta-Johns to promote themselves the way they do on those big billboards around town:

JAYCEES – Remember the good things they do do.

Computers
Probably Are Evil

A Computer Sank My Boat

This started out to be a column about a boat, but it got sunk along the way.

No, it wasn't the boat that got sunk, it was the column, blasted by a single well-aimed shot fired by a computer.

Let me tell you, there are few sinking feelings quite so sinking as the one that comes when the man from tech services stands before your computer terminal, where only minutes before you were launching a perfectly beautiful column, and says, "Bad news. It's lost."

When he does it 18 minutes before deadline, after an editor has already once inquired somewhat impatiently about your progress, then it is time for panic, for grasping desperately for lifelines.

When you have spent much of a day crafting a piece, honing and polishing it into a sleek vessel loaded with humor, insight and deep feeling, it simply isn't possible to jerry-rig it back in an hour or so, especially in a panic.

I am talking real panic here, not mere jitters. I am talking flailing around, gasping, hollering for help. I am talking seeing all the columns of your past flashing before your eyes as you start to go down for the third time.

I knew that I would eventually find myself in this predicament. I sensed it from the moment years ago when I first glimpsed one of these cold instruments in which we all place so much faith nowadays. I knew that I could never trust a machine that turned writing into capricious electrodes capable of disappearing into outer space on a whim. That was why I resisted working on them for years.

"But they are wonderful," people kept telling me.

"No, they aren't," I insisted. "They are cold and calculating and probably evil."

"You will love them once you start working on one," they promised. "They make it so much easier."

"I may work on one," I said, "but I will never love it."

No doubt, the machine was listening.

I could tell that it was out to get me. It strived to confuse me – and succeeded regularly. It was very authoritarian, too, always giving me stern commands and insisting that I carry them out to the letter. "Bad name," it would snap if I didn't do things exactly right.

It was constantly doing little things to hurt me. Dropping a line here. Stealing a few paragraphs there.

For a long time, I wrote my columns in long hand and used the computer only as a device for getting them into the "system," whatever that is. But gradually I got lulled into writing directly on the machine.

"Now tell the truth," my co-workers would say, "you like it, don't you? It's easier, isn't it? Come on, admit it."

"I won't admit any such thing," I'd say, although I had long since begun placing complete faith in it, turning over my precious words to it, expecting it to bring them back tangible, ink on paper, the way words are supposed to be collected.

I should have realized that the machine was simply biding its time, waiting for the right moment to strike. That time came one Tuesday evening. Wednesday's column obliterated, a stream of electrodes making for the outer galaxies, never to be recovered.

The machine seemed to be gloating as it sat glaring "Deleted" to the technicians who were struggling to figure what had gone wrong.

I knew what had happened. It had got me. But I don't give up as easily as it may have thought. This very column is proof that this fight has just begun. Given time, I fully intend to set another version of that boat column asail, even if have to shove it off by hand.

The Message Function

Last year, when we were about to get our new computer system here at the paper, people kept telling me how much I was going to like it.

I was wary. I often don't like things people tell me I'm going to like, especially technical things. Besides, I had just grudgingly gotten used to the old system.

"One thing you're going to love is the message function," people who had experience with the machine told me. "It's wonderful."

I had to admit that the message function sounded promising, maybe even a lot of fun. With it we could send private messages to anybody on our system, which meant to all of the reporters and editors in all of the various departments, even the outlying bureaus such as Raleigh and Eden. We also could send general messages to different departments or to everybody.

A lot of the message function's promise dissipated when I got my computer and discovered that it automatically affixed my name to any message I sent. No anonymous messages. Most I really wanted to send were eliminated right off the bat.

The machine had other drawbacks. Each person has his own secret code word which gives him access to the machine and the ability to send messages. But once you give the machine your secret code (having a secret code is the most fun about the whole thing; I hadn't had one since I was a kid, and nobody would ever guess mine), anybody still can sit down at your machine and send a message and it will go forth with your name attached.

Say you're writing a story and you get up to get a drink of

water without signing off your machine. While you're gone, somebody hurries over and sends an indecent proposal to a young lady across the room, or sends a message to the editor calling him an old fuddy-duddy, which, of course, he is not. Well, I'm sure you can see the consequences of something like that. I mean, if you're not careful, this message function can get you into real trouble, slapped, at the least, if not fired, or hauled into court.

When we first got these computers, I pictured the message function bringing me a lot of fun stuff – snappy repartee, maybe even a risque joke, an invitation to lunch, an occasional compliment. It hasn't quite turned out that way.

About the only private messages I ever get are like this: "The four-legged chicken in Denton is MINE! Jenkins." Mostly, the messages I get are general ones that go to everybody, the ones that used to go on the bulletin board before the message function came along. Somebody's getting married; somebody's having a baby.

There are lots of messages about meetings. Newspapers hold a lot more meetings than they used to, and reporters are expected to attend many of them. Sometimes it seems that meeting is all that editors do. I've heard that editors call meetings to decide whether to go to the bathroom – and if they do decide going is the best course, they prepare agendas to take with them to ensure that they do everything in the proper order and with maximum efficiency. This may not be true.

Sometimes the messages are just pitches: "Friends, the time is here. We need to rally to kick our United Way giving over the goal by – TOMORROW."

Sometimes they are helpful hints: "Gentle readers: in our newspaper's style, a person criticizes someone else; he doesn't 'blast' him. And a candidate campaigns; he doesn't stump." (If a person's criticism extends to gunshot and dynamite, can he blast? Can a one-legged candidate stump? I guess not.)

Sometimes people send out general messages that make you wonder about them.

On October 2nd, a fellow in the features department sent this: "Today is Groucho Marx's birthday, as well as Mohandas Gandhi's. It's the anniversary of the first episode of *The Twilight Zone* and the first 'Peanuts' comic strip. And it's the date that Phileas Fogg made his wager. Thought you'd like to know." A reporter in the High Point bureau used to sign on every day with a general greeting, "Good morning! Have a nice news day!" He had been away from reporting for several years, had just returned to it and he was filled with vigor and enthusiasm. Lately, his greetings have been far less frequent. Must be those High Point news days.

Now and then, intriguing messages come across. Consider this recent series.

Oct. 9 – "BULLETIN: The Imelda Marcos cup is missing from the copy desk. This cup, though it is only plastic and it's cracked, means a lot to the copy desk. It also meant a great deal to Mrs. Marcos. Please let us know if you have any info on its whereabouts."

Oct. 14 – "Ok, the joke is over. Return the Imelda Marcos cup now – no questions asked, no reputations soiled – just put the cup in any copy editor's mailbox – and run."

What is this cup? And why is it so important? Is it some kind of honor, like the America's Cup, and if so, what did the copy desk do to earn it, count shoes? Maybe I'll get a message about it.

Me & My Modem

When sleet started falling in earnest one Friday afternoon, I rushed home from the office in a fit of excitement.

It wasn't just that I didn't want to be trapped in Greensboro. No, this storm was going to give me the chance to write a column on my home computer for the first time and send it to Greensboro by way of the new "modem," which is the gizmo that allows one computer to talk to another over the telephone.

Wonder where they got that word? Modem. It's not in my dictionary, but then my dictionary is nearly as old as I am, and I seriously predate computers.

It sounds vaguely Middle Eastern, doesn't it? If by chance it has some double meaning that is offensive to fundamentalist Moslems I hope that before the ayatollahs dispatch the death squads they will take into consideration that I dislike the term instinctively, use it reluctantly and intend no malice.

My modem, incidentally, isn't new. I bought it nearly a year ago, and Erik installed it in my computer shortly afterwards. But I've never used the thing for the simple reason that I could never figure out how to make it work.

I have trouble with electronic devices. I've had a VCR for more than four years now and I still don't know how to record anything on it. I can't set the timer on the oven or turn off the digital alarm clock in the bedroom. I still have to ask somebody to change my watch when daylight savings time comes and goes. Until a friend with a touch of electronic genius came to my rescue my watch would lapse into infernal and unbearable beeping every midnight and not even throwing it into the commode would stop it, for it is a diver's watch.

This should give you some idea of my level of competence when it comes to such complicated devices as computers and modems.

One of the big reasons that I couldn't figure out the function of my modem is that I have had no more luck mastering computer language, or the gobbledygook that is used in computer instruction manuals, than I did in conquering Latin in high school.

Truth is, as hard as it might have been for Miss Lydia Stronach, my Latin teacher, to believe, bless her soul, I may have had more success with that ancient language that she so loved. With patience and a Latin dictionary, I could at least slog my way through coarse, if not course, translations. But I have yet to encounter a dictionary to help me understand what my computer and its six-inch-thick stack of instruction manuals are trying to tell me.

For that, I depend entirely upon my son, the computer whiz. Erik even majored in computer science his first year at N.C. State, until he discovered that, although they are flashy and seductive, helpful and even necessary in such complicated times, down deep computers are boring.

He became an English major, poor child, but he maintains an interest in computers and uses them regularly. He even knows how to perform such exotic acts as "accessing" computer data banks and other amazing feats of agility by modem, all quite beyond my comprehension.

He had promised to teach me to use my modem, but other things kept coming up. I was in no particular hurry. The main reason I wanted a modem was so that if I got snowed in, as I had many times in the past – last year for five straight days – I would be able to write my column at home and zap it straight into the newspaper's computer.

Cold weather arrived and I still couldn't use my modem. When Erik came home from graduate school at Christmas, my computer had ceased functioning altogether and I had to take it away for repairs. By the time I got it back, Erik was gone again.

Fortunately, January turned balmy and I didn't need

rescue by modem. At month's end, Erik came home for a night and was about to show me how to use my modem when he discovered that an essential program was now missing from my hard disk, whatever that is.

When he returned unexpectedly last weekend to install the program, I wasn't around and missed my big chance to become user friendly with my modem. He left a message, though, telling me to call him so that he could talk me through the process.

That call lasted about two hours, and after many missteps and much confusion and frustration, I actually succeeded in sending a short piece of copy from my computer in my little cabin on my Randolph County hillside straight into the newspaper's big computer in Greensboro.

Oh, the excitement . . .

At the time, of course, I had no idea that in just a few short days, I would have the unbelievable good fortune to get myself iced in and put my new knowledge to a genuine test.

If you are reading this, it's a modem miracle.

The Technological Illiterate

Life's hard enough without waking up one morning to discover that you are a technological illiterate, but that's just what happened to me one Saturday.

I guess I knew it all along. It's just not one of those things that you wake up asking yourself every day: "Am I or am I not technologically literate?"

The reason I asked it Saturday was because such questions were being pondered at a scientific conference in Baltimore that weekend.

One of the matters taken up was a recent poll for the National Science Foundation that had some conference participants disturbed. The poll was designed to find out how well-informed people are about technological issues.

One result of the poll that had the scientific folks concerned was the finding that 76 percent of those surveyed believed that "there are good ways of treating sickness that medical science does not recognize."

I'm surprised that the percentage wasn't considerably higher because everybody knows that wearing a copper bracelet will cure arthritis, bursitis and various other ailments of the bones and joints. And it is a proven fact that snuff juice will take the swelling out of a bee sting.

Beyond that, I know from personal experience that if you will hold a piece of paper over a wart, spit on the paper and mail it to somebody you don't like, that person will get your wart. That is a whole lot easier and cheaper than having some doctor cut it out, even if it does make you technologically illiterate to do it.

Another finding that had the conference crowd worked up

is that 43 percent believed that UFOs are really spaceships from other worlds.

I'm not sure how I feel about that, because I've never seen a UFO myself. But I once interviewed a man in Trinity who claimed that a UFO had hit his trailer and landed in his yard, and sure enough, his trailer had a dent in the top and there was a big round spot burned in his grass.

I also once heard about a woman who, after leaving a night spot at High Rock Lake, was picked up by four-armed creatures in a spaceship and enticed to drink strange potions that caused her to do exotic dances all night to the music of Roy Acuff – and her husband believed her.

Forty-one percent of those polled thought that rocket launchings and space activities have caused changes in the weather. Well, you have to admit that we've been having some strange weather ever since they started that stuff, but I think it goes back before rockets to when jet planes started leaving all those lines across the sky. I don't see how that could help but mess things up.

One thing I'm sure of is that the moon landings didn't have anything to do with it because I have in my possession certain documents sent to me by a man in Haw River that show without doubt that those alleged moon landings never took place and actually were staged in the desert in Nevada to fool people.

Some findings of the poll pleased the science foundation, but I am personally doubtful about these results. On these matters, I think most of the people either were lying or they didn't really understand the question.

For example, 82 percent claimed to have a clear or general understanding of radiation. How can you have an understanding of something you can't see or feel? I think most people were lying about that so they wouldn't appear dumb.

In all my life, I've only met one person who claimed to have a clear understanding of radiation and she believed that those funny looking towers on top of the Southern Bell building in downtown Greensboro were sending out deadly rays designed to kill us all.

One question clearly had to have been misunderstood, because 67 percent said they had a clear or general understanding of how a telephone works. I'm sure they must've thought the questioner was asking whether they had an understanding of how to push the buttons or dial the numbers to make a call. Telephones, after all, defy the laws of nature, and everybody should be aware of that. I mean, how can my voice jump onto a wire, run across town and jump into your ear at the same moment I speak?

To complicate matters even more, I can speak into two phones at once, and the person at the end of one line can be just across town while the person on the other line is thouands of miles across the country and both will hear me at the same instant. You know it would take longer for a voice to run all the way across the country than it would just to run across town. Common sense tells you that.

Nobody can really understand how a telephone works. Even Alexander Graham Bell knew it was impossible.

Everybody knows that the first full message Bell spoke over his invention was to his assistant Thomas Watson in another room: "'Watson, come here, I need you."

What a lot of people don't know is Bell's startled response when Watson actually came: "Dadgum, it must be magic."

That's the only explanation for how a telephone works. Nobody really understands magic, I don't care what they say. And if that makes me a technological illiterate, so be it.

Doing My Civic Duties

AUTOGRAPHS
BY THE
AUTHOR

The Early Bird Gets Confused

I have never been an early riser. Nine o'clock is an early hour for getting up, as far as I'm concerned. Ten is even better.

For me to get up before 7:00, I have to have a powerful reason. I might, for example, get up at such an hour to watch Bo Derek ride a horse naked around my patio, but it would be a close call.

So why was it that 5:30 Tuesday morning found me stumbling numbly from bed, after getting to sleep about 1:00 and being kept awake much of the intervening time by a ferocious storm?

Call it patriotic duty.

I was getting up to vote.

Now we all know that there is no requirement that one must arise at such an uncivilized hour to vote. I was doing it because I had inadvertently boxed myself in on voting day.

I was supposed to be on the *Good Morning Show* with my friend Lee Kinard that morning and had to be at the TV station at 7:15. I had scheduled an interview that evening at 7:00. I didn't want to have to make an hour-and-a-half round trip back home to Randolph County during the day just to vote.

So I decided to get up at 5:30, be at the polls when they opened at 6:30, then head for the TV station and hope I got there on time. Everything hinged on being able to vote quickly, and I knew that just reading through the list of gubernatorial candidates to find my choice would be at least a five minute job.

I arrived at the polls at exactly 6:28, as fresh as a single cup of lukewarm coffee, downed on the drive, could make me. I was pleased to see no line. Not another soul, in fact.

I was the very first voter to appear in my precinct, and I followed the red "Vote Here" signs into a large room where a small group of poll workers was milling around looking confused. They were looking that way, I soon discovered, because that was precisely the condition they were in.

Just to let the group know that a certified voter had appeared to perform his solemn duty, I asked what time the polls opened.

"Well, they're supposed to open at 6:30, but we're not ready yet," somebody told me.

The voting machines were not yet prepared and nobody seemed exactly sure of his or her function.

"Before, we had a list of just what we were supposed to do," one woman said, looking lost.

I stood for several minutes watching the chaos, wondering whether I should leave and make the long trip back later, or wait a little longer and risk having to call Lee Kinard and tell him he'd have to send the Sky 2 helicopter for me if he wanted me to make the show.

Meanwhile, somebody remembered that the workers had to take an oath, but the woman who was supposed to bring it forgot. Much discussion ensued about this before it was decided that they would make up the oath. They placed their hands on a Bible and swore to all sorts of things that sounded somber and right.

"Oh, Lord," I heard one of the workers say, glancing at me, "this will probably end up in his column."

Finally, after much ado, one machine was deemed fit for service. Two guys instructed in finding my name in the fat registration book and checking my attendance in the proper block performed admirably. A woman again asked my name and party affiliation and wrote it in another book.

"I'm not the one who's supposed to be doing this," she said.

She picked up a yellow slip of paper.

"Now you're supposed to get this and hand it to me over there," she said, handing me the slip, then taking it back, "so I'll just keep it."

We walked to the voting machine and I stepped inside while she fiddled and pushed buttons on the side.

"OK," she said.

I took hold of the handle that is supposed to close the curtains and make the machine ready to receive votes. It wouldn't budge.

"It won't close," I said.

She pressed and fiddled some more. "Try it again."

I tried. Nothing doing.

She stepped inside and gave the handle a sound whack. Still no go.

I stepped out; the other workers gathered around and we contemplated the situation. Several suggestions were bandied about. I even offered a few myself, although I am a mechanical moron.

Somebody got out an instruction book and we went over it step by step. The problem seemed to be in the positioning of key slot No. 2, but it wouldn't work in any position.

While we were mulling this, two other voters had arrived and stood watching us with bewilderment.

Finally, it was decided that somebody with expertise would have to be fetched from the courthouse, a block away. I glanced nervously at the clock. Only a miracle could deliver me to the TV station on time now.

"We've got to let these people vote," somebody said.

"Well, we can let them use those curbside ballots," said a woman who appeared to be in charge.,

I was handed a long white ballot, which I hurriedly marked. Then I realized that it didn't include all the races.

"Oh," said a woman I asked about it, "I was supposed to give you some of these. "

This time I got a handful of ballots, all different colors. I was marking those when I heard somebody say, "You know, we don't have a ballot box. "

"Look," I said, handing my folded ballots to one of the women, "I'm just going to trust you with these."

I left the place at a dead run and made it to the TV station in the nick of time, but I was a nervous wreck. Just goes to prove that it doesn't pay to get up early.

Exploring the Desktop Thicket

The calls and letters have been coming for weeks, all with the same demand.

"Why are you depriving us?" they wanted to know. "Twice a year, in winter and summer, we wait for that glorious day when you clean off your desk and tell us about all the wondrous things you have found. Yet this summer we were denied that great privilege and pleasure. How do you expect us to go on? Why are you doing this to us? Is there no mercy in your heart?"

Pressure like that is more than I can bear, and I saw no alternative but to bow to it. Yet I kept putting it off only partly because the clutter had grown to unprecedented proportions.

Cleaning off the desk requires facing failure and lack of responsibility. It means confronting the letters that never were answered, the calls that somehow didn't get returned, the promises that went unkept. One of the first things I found was a packet of photographs I promised to return months ago.

Beyond that, such a task could prove downright dangerous. You never know what may have taken up abode in such a place. A guy could get snakebitten in a thicket like that.

Inevitably, the work proves puzzling, Take this electrical cord that I found, a substantial gadget going under the trade name Snapit. But it is less than a foot long and plugged into itself, like a dog biting its tail. What use could it have? And what am I doing with it?

And how do I get all these pen caps? There must be 50 of them scattered through the debris, all without pens. What happened to the pens? Surely people must come and dump boxes of pen caps on my desk to confound me.

Any foray into this phenomenal muddle usually produces some disappointment. Such certainly was the case when I came upon a letter addressed, "Dear Cow Chip Throwing Contestant."

It had to do with an event held the 28th of September in Yanceyville in conjunction with the fourth annual Bright Leaf Hoedown. A celebrity event, it was billed. I was invited to be one of the contestants. I had to miss it because I was on vacation, but I was not happy about it.

Twenty years of writing a column surely would have given me an edge in a contest of that sort.

I also came upon documentation of another event that I had to miss this summer, this one due to work. "1959 THS Class Reunion Enjoyable Time, Great Success," read the headline on this report.

The Thomasville High School Class of '59 was my class, if I could be said to have one. I did not graduate with them, having flunked too many subjects to be allowed that honor, but I made my way through most of 12 years of schooling with many of them.

The reunion, the 26th, was held June 29th. It was the 26th because somebody failed to organize the 25th.

Peggy Truelove greeted arrivals in poodle skirt and bobby socks, and don't ask me what a poodle skirt is. Charles Tysinger gave a welcoming '50s slide show with Elvis music for background.

The program included a presentation entitled "The Garden" and an inspirational talk of an undescribed nature. I hope it was not on the line of the inspirational talks I received so frequently from W.S. Horton, our beleaguered principal.

Everybody signed a card for Mr. Horton, incidentally, as well as for teachers who managed to survive the Class of '59.

Platters songs were played, along with others of a more lively nature, I take it, for according to the report "each and everyone enjoyed renewing friendships, rock, rolling, and twisting and later soaking their 'shagged out' feet in tubs of hot water."

That is not exactly a pretty mental picture, all my classmates sitting around soaking their feet. Another little item in that report bothered me, too. It was the one about all the bragging going on about children and grandchildren.

Now that I think about it, I'm not so sure that I regret missing that affair. I think I'd have felt out of place in that crowd of old-timers.

Well, as usual, here I am almost out of space, and I haven't even gotten to some of the more unusual things that I found this time.

Like this mail order catalog ad for scratch-and-sniff watches, raspberry, banana and ice mint.

And all these odd little newspaper clippings.

Here's an ad for the Short Folks Dating Club appealing for "ladies who enjoy the pleasures of shorter men (or would like to learn)."

A story I tore from some paper claims that people who watch a lot of TV are fatter than those who don't, although I'm not sure what that proves.

And consider this story out of China: "'Doctors in Shandong Province have successfully rebuilt a human nose using a portion of a pig's ear, the *China Daily* reported Tuesday.

"The patient is described as a young peasant whose nose was bitten off by a rat 25 years ago, the paper said. Ten months after the operation the procedure has been declared a total success, with the doctors reporting that the man can breathe and smell perfectly."

OK, sure, but is he bad to root?

The Stool Shortage

Leave it to me to uncover problems that the rest of the world is blissfully ignorant of.

The stool shortage, for example.

I might not have learned about this problem myself, if not for a peculiarity of mine.

The nature of my work requires – demands – that I occasionally speak before one group or another. I do not like this and make no secret of it. I do all that I can to avoid it, but sometimes I have to do it anyway.

In attempting to analyze why I dislike speaking so much, I came up with a theory that it might have something to do with the awkwardness and unnaturalness of standing in front of a group of sitting people. This is aggravated in my case because I am tall and the average lectern is made to accommodate people half my height. This requires me to lean forward to reach the microphone. That not only gives me a humped-over look but makes me feel that I am about to fall on my face literally as well as figuratively.

I had the thought that if I could sit on a stool, it might make speaking easier. For one thing, it would make me about the right height for the microphone. It also would put some solid support beneath me, and perhaps put me a little more at ease. There is something nice and casual about perching on a stool.

If nothing else, it would at least allow me to hold my legs apart and keep my knees from banging together and setting up a racket loud enough to interrupt my talk.

Anyway, I tried it and found it to my liking. I still didn't like speaking, but I didn't like it just a little less than when I had to stand to do it.

This immediately created problems, however. When it became impossible to avoid accepting a speaking invitation, I started telling the people requesting my dubious elocution that I would require a stool on which to elocute.

After a pause, during which, I'm sure, they were preparing themselves for even weirder demands and beginning to think that they should have tried for Arlo Lassen or Frank Deal, they always say that will be no problem at all. They will have a stool at my disposal when I arrive.

What these people don't know about, of course, is the stool shortage. Don't ask me why, but it is all but impossible to find a good serviceable stool at any of the varied institutions where the crime of public speaking is apt to be inflicted. I know this from hard experience.

A good example of what happens occurred last week when I arrived to speak at Guilford College, fulfilling a promise made many months ago only because the date of the event seemed so far away when I agreed to come that I figured I might be dead by the time it arrived. Ann Deagon, the poet and novelist who arranged my visit, told me, of course, that finding a stool would be no problem.

I arrived to find Ann smiling apologetically. The reason sat at the front of the hall: a dinky little wooden stool that might have served handily for milking but was hardly a foundation for a lanky and insecure speaker. Ann said she had scavenged the whole campus just to find that sawed-off excuse for a stool, a story I'd heard many times before.

I sat on it, just to see if it might do, only to have Ann laugh and say, "You look like a grasshopper!"

I did not despair for I was prepared, because I knew what Ann did not: something is happening to all of the legitimate stools in this country. That's why I always pack a stool in the back of my car whenever I go to make a talk, despite all of the assurances of my hosts. All I had to do was go and fetch it.

I started carrying my own stool after I showed up for several talks only to learn that people who had promised me stools had not been able to produce them, despite frantic last-minute searches, and I ended up having to deliver my talk even more nervously than usual, perched precariously on boxes and stepladders and rickety tabletops.

However, carrying around your own stool is not something that can be done without risk of peril, I'm sorry to report. Four times in the past six months or so, while leaving places where I have spoken – once at a fancy hotel, once at a restaurant, twice at colleges – I have been accosted by people who suspected me of stealing a stool.

Each time, it took a far better speech than I delivered on the stool to keep these suspicious proprietors from calling the cops.

Maybe that is the reason for the shortage. Maybe some maniacal thief is going around making off with all the stools.

But just because a guy is leaving a public building carrying a stool does not necessarily make him a thief. If he is tall and lanky and wearing an expression of great relief, he may only have been the reluctant speaker of the evening.

Speaking to the Senior Set

For a fellow just getting uneasily settled into middle age, I get around to a lot of senior citizen affairs.

The reason is simple enough. I have trouble saying no to old ladies pleading over the telephone. Could you tell somebody who sounds like your grandmother to buzz off?

One thing that many people do after they enter their twilight years and check out of the hectic mainstream of commerce is organize. They get together in what are called senior citizen groups. It gets them out of the house, lets them mingle with people and get involved in things, helps keep the vital juices flowing.

The problem is that these meetings must have some sort of form, and that usually means a program, which inevitably results in a speaker – if one can be lassoed and hogtied, or otherwise cajoled into coming.

More often than not, these speakers are apt to be cheerful preachers who remind the oldtimers of their mortality and the rather imminent consequences of it. After suffering through preachers week after week, some of these groups get desperate enough to seek another type of speaker, and an old lady who sounds like my grandmother and has the plea-making abilities to win an acquittal for a mass murderer is assigned to call me.

If I am not quick enough that day to think up an immediate excuse that would prevent me from coming, and if I can't convince this grandmotherly voice that Jim Jenkins would make a far better speaker ("We had him last week," they always say), I end up agreeing to come and be the program, although making talks is about as much pleasure for me as sitting through an opera or a city council meeting.

After you have been the speaker at a few senior citizen groups, you become wary enough to inquire whether you will be put on before or after the business session. Before is essential. I have sat through some business sessions at these meetings that went on so long that I began to wonder if some of the members would live long enough to hear me talk.

You never know what's apt to come up during these business sessions. I once sat through a roll call that threatened to break into a cat fight.

Roll call, by the way, can be a tedious affair indeed if the group is a large one, especially considering that some members are hard of hearing ("What did he say?" a man at the back of the room loudly asked a friend at one meeting when I got up to speak and asked if everybody could hear.)

At one meeting I attended, the secretary finished a long roll call, fraught with difficulties, only to have a woman speak up and say, "You didn't call Myrtle Johnson, did you?"

"I think I did."

"No you didn't. I was listening and I didn't hear it."

"I've got a check by her name," the secretary said, glaring at the challenger.

"Well, you didn't call it," she said, glaring back.

"Did too."

"Didn't."

I have sat through long reports by treasurers that concluded with a balance of $1.69, and I have even had to help make change during the collection of dues.

I once endured a reading of the minutes that carefully included every detail of what had been said by the preacher who was the previous week's speaker. If you belonged to that group, you really only needed to attend every other week, because you got a double dose every trip.

Another drawn-out part of the business session can be the report on the sick and hospitalized. Sit through a couple of these and you might get the idea that shingles is rampant.

At one meeting I attended, devotions preceded the business session, and after the reading, songbooks were passed around and it was announced that we would sing the first two verses of a certain hymn, accompanied by an accordian-playing member.

The accordian player was in her upper 80s or early 90s but she squeezed with authority. We finished the two verses and she squeezed right into the third. We went ahead with that one and she launched into the fourth. We stumbled through all six verses and she played right on while we all stood wondering what to do next. Finally, somebody punched her with an authority equal to her playing and she stopped in midverse and sat down.

Since I began insisting on talking before the business session, I haven't had to suffer through this sort of thing, but at one meeting I attended, the president did take up a discussion of the upcoming Christmas dinner before I spoke. This evolved into a vote on the question: Will the main dish be turkey with dressing and gravy or ham with raisin sauce.

"Well," said the president after the show of hands, "the ham has it. And now we'll introduce our speaker."

My Network TV Premiere

I admit that I was getting a little anxious as the day drew nearer. For one of the few times in my life, I was even thinking about what I should wear.

Should I go for the hayseedy, country look? Say jeans, a denim shirt and a John Deere hat? Maybe chewing on a straw? No doubt, that's what they would be expecting. Should I throw them a little off-balance by showing up with a casual, preppy look? What about a suit?

No, a suit definitely would be going too far. Besides, I might get some sauce spots on it that wouldn't come out. Then what would I wear to weddings and funerals?

No question about it, though, when you're faced with your first appearance on a major TV network, you want to do what you can to make a good impression. I mean, you never know where something like that can lead. Fame and fortune, or at least opportunity, could be lying out there somewhere just waiting for your appearance.

The beginnings of this anxiety go back a month or so to a day when I got a call from a pleasant woman who identified herself as an agent of CBS News. She had heard, she said, that I might know something about barbecue.

"The world's foremost authority," I said in my modest and unassuming way.

"That's what I'd heard," she said sweetly.

She went on to say that the network was planning to bring its *CBS This Morning* show to North Carolina, and since barbecue is so integral to the state, CBS wanted to tell the nation about it. The show just needed somebody knowledgeable to talk about it, maybe even cook some barbecue to show the folks, whip up some sauces right on the air. Clearly, I was their man.

It was a noble thing that they were doing, I said in my most professional manner, and, of course, I would be happy to do whatever I could to help. Then I calmly hung up and leaped from my chair shouting, "I'm going to be on CBS Morning News!"

With Kathleen Sullivan?" a colleague asked, obviously impressed.

"I don't know," I said, "is she on that show?" Not only was she on it, I learned, but she is supposed to be, as Dave Letterman might say, "one fabulous babe."

I am to be forgiven for not knowing who Kathleen was because I have never seen this particular show. For one thing, it comes on at an ungodly hour when no sane or civilized person is about. For another, it's not on any station that I can get on my TV.

Nonetheless, for the next few days I swaggered around talking about my upcoming appearance and how Kathleen probably would fall into a swoon over my performance, maybe even demand that I join the show as co-host.

In the coming weeks, the plan of my appearance was hashed out. Professionals would cook the barbecue. I would talk about it and whip up some sauces. Then Dennis Rogers, a scribbler for a Raleigh newspaper, and I would debate the merits of Eastern vs. Lexington styles.

I didn't really mind this guy Rogers horning in on my spot. We'd had these debates on TV before. The man doesn't know barbecue from bean sprouts. I would quickly make minced meat of him, so to speak. All the more with which to impress Kathleen.

The show was to be live on Monday, April 25. The week before my appearance, CBS called to confirm it. I should come to Raleigh on Sunday evening. A room would be awaiting me at a fancy hotel. There would be a cocktail party with Kathleen and other notables. At 6:00 the next morning, a limousine would take me for rehearsals. The show would go on at 7:00.

I called all around the country telling friends and family to be sure to watch.

"This is not going to be like that Letterman deal is it?" my son, Erik, asked when I called to tell him. A year or so ago, a staff member of the *Late Night* show on NBC told me that David Letterman was going to mention one of my books on his show. Erik invited all of his friends to his dorm room for a *Late Night* party to watch. Letterman never mentioned me or the book.

"Oh, no," I said. "I'm on for sure this time."

This week, with anxiety building, I assembled ingredients and utensils and practiced making sauces. I rehearsed what I would say and thought up all sorts of clever repartee to exchange with Kathleen. Friday, after spending the morning taking outfits out of my closet and mulling over them, I came to work to find an alien New York voice on my answering machine.

"I have the unfortunate chore of calling to tell you that because we've added a business segment to our broadcast on Monday we have dropped the barbecue segment," it said. "So though it would have been wonderful to have you, we're sorry..."

"A business segment," I said, commiserating with Rogers over the telephone. "Can you imagine that? I guess we know now why CBS is in last position."

"What's even worse," he said, "is that my ex-wife works for the company they're going to feature."

A scumbag network, CBS, we agreed. With an especially boring morning news show.

"The way I look at it, it's Kathleen's loss, not ours," Rogers said.

"Yeah," I said. "Me, too."

The Perils of the Autograph Party

Anytime book writers, poor wretches, get together, one subject almost certain to come up is autograph sessions.

Maybe that's because misery has such a way of clinging to memory.

Sometimes I think that the Lord must have created autograph parties just to keep writers humble.

Don't get me wrong. Autograph parties can be sweet experiences, not only enjoyable but exhilarating – if people show up and buy your book – and I've had a few of those. Unfortunately, that usually isn't the case.

I suppose there are people who write books – television or movie stars, maybe, big-name politicians or repeat best-seller authors – who have huge crowds turn out for signing parties. But for the run-of-the-list writer, autographings are more apt to be lonely, humiliating and long-remembered affairs.

Heartbreaking stories abound. And like all the other writers I know, I think I've suffered more than my share.

A couple of years ago, I drove all the way to Myrtle Beach at my own expense for no other purpose than to present myself at one of these to-dos.

Sold one book.

And that was to a fellow who wandered innocently into the store to kill some time and was embarrassed into buying one, although he clearly had no interest in it, when he discovered that he was the only person who had showed up for this grand occasion. I'm sure he left cursing himself for his bad timing and lack of courage for not being able to say no.

That one was not so bad as some, though. I've had several when I didn't sell any books at all.

One of these was my very first autographing nearly eight years ago. I did a television interview in Charlotte and was immediately whisked to a big downtown department store to await the admiring throngs.

My books were displayed on a counter next to the stairway leading to the lunchroom, the most heavily trafficked spot in the store. And there I perched on a stool for two hours during the midday rush, while hundreds of people scurried by ignoring me.

The young woman in charge of the book department had recently been transferred from lingerie and I could tell her heart really wasn't in books. She obviously felt sorry for me and took it upon herself to keep me entertained. Over the next hour, we exhausted every conversational subject known, including the intricacies of the lingerie trade, and lapsed into a fidgety silence for the second half of the ordeal.

Just as I was getting ready to leave, a man in a topcoat stopped, picked up one of my books and thumbed through it. I brightened. "Better let me fix you up one of those," I said, mustering all my charm. "I'm just getting ready to leave.

"Personally," he said, putting down the book, "I think you look ridiculous sitting there."

Just goes to prove that you look like you feel, I guess.

A few years back I was the guest of honor at the grand opening of a book store in a town in the western part of the state that previously had been devoid of such cultural niceties. The woman who owned the store was so enthusiastic that she had brought in a radio station disc jockey to do a live remote broadcast of the festivities.

The trouble was that the festivities were somewhat scant. They consisted of a few people browsing through the magazines and paperbacks and a couple of junior high girls flirting with the DJ.

I sat with poised pen, while the DJ struggled vainly to make the event sound as exciting as a high-school football game and the store owner frantically called all of her relatives, friends and neighbors imploring them to at least come and say hello to ease some of the embarrassment.

Most of the people she called were too smart to get involved, but she did convince one young employee to come buy a book, no doubt under threat of her job. I would have been pleased about that if the DJ hadn't got so excited describing the transaction that I was afraid he might have a stroke and I'd have to do the last hour of his broadcast alone.

Perhaps my most memorable autographing, though, was at a Charlotte shopping mall when my first book came out. That book was about the rough and tumble world of stock car racing.

I arrived at the big department store to find that a place had been arranged for me on the busiest aisle in the store. My books were stacked on a dainty white desk with curved legs. I was to sit behind it on a fragile stool with a pink cushion.

I had been sitting there completely ignored for about 20 minutes when a young couple came up the aisle and headed straight toward me, smiling.

"This is just what we've been looking for," the young man said.

I stood, flooded with gratitude. "Well, I'm sure glad," I said, taking up my pen.

"How much is this desk?" the young woman said, coming around to pull out the drawer.

Awards and Honors

AWARD

FOR THE
COMMON MAN

Honoring the Common Man

My attention was caught this week by a newspaper headline that said, "Awards to honor 'the common man.'"

The story beneath the headline was by The Associated Press out of Raleigh. It said that the Z. Smith Reynolds Foundation had announced a new series of awards honoring "the common man."

Foundation President Smith Bagley was quoted as saying: "The greatness of North Carolina is founded not on the few prominent leaders who have come forth from time to time, but on the common man, whose contributions to the common good are woven into the lasting fabric of this state. That is the greatness of our society – hard work and good ideas that emanate from the grass-roots level...."

This certainly is an uncommon thing that the foundation is doing, and I commend them for it. It's about time somebody came up with some awards for ordinary people who graze through life as members of the common herd, utterly without distinction.

But I can see a few problems with it.

First, I am curious as to just how you would go about picking a winner. How do you distinguish one common man from another? If a common man does something to distinguish himself, doesn't it raise him above the herd, thereby making him ineligible for a common man award?

It seems to me that about the only way to do it would be to hold a lottery in which only the names of common people are entered. But how would you determine just whose name to put into the pot? Who would do the picking? What would be the criteria? How do you even find out about a common person?

With all the common people in this state, surely you would miss some deserving ones who ought to be in the drawing

Maybe the best way to do it would be to let common people enter themselves. But then you'd probably end up with a lot of deejays and Jaycees and other glory seekers trying to slip into the competition.

Even with a successful lottery, I still can see all kind of problems developing.

What if some sore loser claimed that the winner wasn't common enough, that he, the loser, indeed was far more common and should have received the award? I don't know how they'd deal with something like that.

But let's assume that everything works out all right and a winner is chosen without objection. Common sense would tell you that the mere act of singling out such an individual suddenly makes him special and no longer common.

How could such a distinguished person in good faith keep an award designed for the common man? Surely, he'd have to do the honorable thing and relinquish it. I can see a vicious cycle developing here.

Another thing I'm curious about is exactly what the award will say. "For distinguished commonness"? "Outstandingly common"? "In recognition of excessive commonness"? "Uncommonly common"? "As common as you can get"? That brings up another matter. Some people might not take kindly to being named winner of an award for commonness. Who among us has not seen somebody look down his nose at another person and sniff, "Oh, he's just common." One of the definitions of the word, after all, is "ill-bred, not refined in behavior or style" (I'm sure that's not what the foundation wants to honor, or it would have announced just another award for newspaper columnists).

Anyway, it would be embarrassing if the winner showed up at the awards ceremony, punched Smith Bagley in the nose and stalked off in a huff. That isn't likely to happen, I expect, because the foundation has had the uncommon foresight to sweeten the award with $25,000 in common United States currency.

Hand that kind of money to a common man and what's he apt to do?

Why, no doubt he'll go right out and blow it trying to set himself apart from the common folks. Probably buy a four-wheel drive Mercedes, jack it up in the air and put them big cruncher wheels on it.

You know, the more I think about it, an award for the common man seems to be somehow self-defeating. But if the foundation decides to go ahead and start giving it, I just want to remind them that I have a wide reputation for being about as common as they come.

Overooking-lay Enius-gay

Once again I have been overlooked, sad to say. I'm beginning to suspect that the powers that be may doubt my genius.

Otherwise, surely the MacArthur Foundation would have called by now.

That foundation called 32 others this week to tell them that they are getting big chunks of money, no strings attached, for the next five years, not to mention full health insurance for that period. The grants ranged from $190,000 to $375,000.

The idea of the awards, which were funded by an eccentric billionaire insurance guy, is to allow people of genius or particular promise time to work on whatever they choose without worrying about money. But they don't have to work if they don't want to. They can travel or just lie around and squander the whole bundle. Nobody demands an accounting.

This is the kind of deal I have been looking for all my life, but so far I have been unable to attract the attention of the committee that selects the recipients. The whole process is very secret, and nobody can nominate you except for 100 anonymous sources who serve for only a year at a time.

From scanning this year's list of winners, I have concluded that whatever you do should sound important if you want one of these anonymous sources to take note of you. It probably isn't enough to have a particular genius for hog calling or shad scaling, nor would it likely do you much good to show great promise as, say, a commercial popcorn popper.

You would be far better off to be a theoretical physicist trying to tie nature's forces together into one neat theory. Or a philologist studying South American Indian traditions. Or an evolutionary ecologist working on "problems of parental investment and control of sex ratio." Or an endocrinologist studying stress-related disorders in wild baboons. Or even the guy who designed a camera to go to Mars. People who do all of these things got calls from the foundation this year.

Scientists. Sociologists. Artists. Writers. Such are the people who catch the eye of the anonymous sources. Your average Tom's Toasted Peanuts routeman doesn't have much of a chance, although he certainly adds a great deal of pleasure, comfort and nutrition to my life.

Since I fit loosely into one of these categories of favored recipients, I've held on to some slight hope of being recognized by the foundation. Of course, I've gone along for years thinking that Ed McMahon is going to call any day, too.

But just because no local newspaper columnist with a strong concern for barbecue standards has yet won a MacArthur award is no reason to give up hope, not when writers of other sorts are getting these things right and left. At least nine writers were among the 32 people who got calls from the foundation this week. One, who got $330,000, was described as an avant-garde writer known for his social, philosophical and linguistic concerns. This probably means that he writes stuff that nobody can understand but would never admit out of fear of being considered less than brilliant or avant-garde.

I can write gibberish, too, and I think I've shown great promise at it on some occasions. Indeed, some have expressed the opinion that I may verge on genius at this speciality. And I am not without my own deep social, philosophical and linguistic concerns. Why, just the other day I was ondering-way y-whay obody-nay alks-tay ig-pay atin-lay any-way-or-may.

One of the best ways to get a MacArthur grant apparently is to call yourself a poet. Four poets were blessed this year. One, who got $245,000, is described as a "meditative poet," which probably means that he thinks about writing poetry a whole lot more than he does it. I can think about writing poetry with the best.

Another poet, who got $265,000, writes about the American landscape, culture and heritage. I have done some verse in this area myself, but the committee must have overlooked my "Ballad of John Jenrette" and my "Ode to the Chigger." Too bad.

For a while, I thought that the reason I was being overlooked by the foundation was because of where I live. I doubt that any of the anonymous sources who nominate people would be apt to look into a backwater such as Randolph County.

Yet this year some guy from Porcupine, South Dakota, got $210,000 for trying to improve the economy of remote Indian reservations. I have been to Porcupine, South Dakota, and if I lived there and somebody called and told me they were giving me $210,000, I doubt that I would remain in Porcupine any longer than it took for the check to clear.

But if the foundation could just find it in its heart to grant me $60,000 or $70,000 a year for the next five years, I'd swear that I could find some important work to do in Randolph County. Maybe I could translate avant-garde poetry into pig Latin. Or better yet, study the stress-related disorders of wild 'possums trying to cross country roads. If only I could get through to one of those anonymous sources.

Me and Mr. Tacky

Billy "Mr. 8:55" Shepherd was baffled and inconsolable.
"Me tacky?" he said.

"I don't understand it either, Billy," I said.

"Why did they pick on me and you?" he asked plaintively.
"I'm a nice boy."

Billy, who is famous for the operating hours at his carpet
store – 8:55 to 8:55 – turned to a salesman by the name of Carl
Rook who was calling on him.

"Do you think we're tacky?" he asked.

Carl shifted a toothpick from one side of his mouth to the
other and paused diplomatically.

"Well . . ." he said.

Billy didn't wait for the rest of the answer.

"I think that was just plumb tacky of them to do that," he
said to me. "I thought you would've had enough pull up there
to keep them from doing something like that."

What had Billy so upset was a big spread in the Life &
Leisure section of the newspaper where I work that was
headlined "Now That's TACKY!" In it, readers were allowed
to express themselves about what is tacky.

They named such things as using toothpicks in public,
setting up toilet fixtures as lawn ornaments, leaving Christmas
lights up all year, chewing tobacco, using bad grammar and
driving jacked-up cars. They even named a lot of people,
including Bob "We're Dealin" Dunn, Frank "The Joker"
Deal, Lee "The Opinion" Kinard, Aunt "Possum Breath"
Eloise, Jesse "Senator No" Helms, MayCay "Oh That White
Bathing Suit" Beeler, and, of course, me and Billy.

"At least you know why they called you tacky," I said to

Billy. "They didn't list any reasons for putting me on the list. Not even a hint. I don't know whether it's because I drive an old beat-up car without any hubcaps or because I like barbecue and collards, or what."

"Look at the way you dress," Billy said. "You don't exactly dress nice like me." Billy looked like all of the cool guys did when I was back in high school, right down to the penny loafers. A smooth dresser, no doubt about it.

"But most of my jeans don't have holes," I said.

The reason Billy made the list was because of his radio commercials. He sings in them ("My name is Bill-ee Shep-ERRRD, and I own a car-pet store."). The person who nominated him to the list had the audacity to assail Billy's singing. I knew that hurt Billy's feelings. He takes a lot of pride in his music.

Some years back when Billy was scheduled to sing "Take Me Out To The Ball Game" before a charity softball game featuring a lot of Nashville stars, he practiced for weeks beforehand. Seven thousand people turned out for the event at Memorial Stadium, and Billy was very nervous.

Halfway through his song, as I recall, he was arrested for impersonating a singer. There's just not much respect for true artists anymore.

"I don't think those people knew who I was," Billy recalled the other day. "I think they thought I was one of those country music stars."

But back to this tacky business that had stirred Billy into such an indignant state.

He thought that those of us who had been proclaimed tacky ought to get together and protest.

"What would we do?" I asked. "Get Bob Dunn to jump off a sign? I guess we could get Frank Deal to go up to the paper and tell jokes until the responsible editors were whipped into submission and agreed to a retraction. Shouldn't take long. Maybe you could sing to 'em, Billy."

Billy said the least we could do was form a tacky club for all the people who got named. We could get together regularly and just wallow in tackiness. I said I was all for it if we could get MayCay to wear that white bathing suit to the meetings.

Billy said that he was going to mount his own little protest by putting his Christmas lights back up, hanging some velvet paintings inside, setting out some flower boxes with plastic poinsettias in them and arraying some ceramic animals and maybe a toilet bowl on the yard in front of his store. He might even temporarily jack up his Cadillac with the "Mr. 8:55" license tag on it.

Then he'd hold a tacky sale. Why, it might be even bigger than his famous hole-in-the-floor sale.

Sounded like a good idea to me, I told him.

"By the way," Billy said. "You need any carpet? I got some real nice remnants."

"I don't know, Billy," I said. "I don't see anything tacky enough for me."

Dr. of Obfuscation

I guess it's a good thing that I didn't get very far in college. If I had, I might have been tempted to go all the way and try to get one of those highfalutin' degrees so that I could call myself Dr. Bledsoe.

I would have been a miserable failure. Even if I had managed to squeak through the courses required, I'm sure I would have been stopped dead by the dissertation. I might have been able to write one, with heaven's help, but even if through such a miracle I did, I know that I never would have been able to come up with an acceptable title for the thing.

Having an important sounding title must be the most important part of a dissertation. Otherwise, surely, nobody would hang such convoluted handles on anything.

This realization came to me one weekend while I was attending the commencement at N.C. State University. The program not only offered the names, hometowns and fields of study of all the people receiving doctoral degrees, it also listed the titles of their dissertations. That's one reason the program ran to 130 pages.

During some of the ebbs in the pomp and speechifying, I amused myself by reading these titles. Or maybe I should say by trying to read these titles. Most of them just left my brain tangled in knots.

What on earth, I wondered, would "A Comparative Analysis Between the Effectiveness of Conventional and Modular Instruction in Teaching Students with Varied Learning Styles and Individual Differences, Enrolled in High School Industrial Arts Manufacturing" possibly be about? I'll never know, but it got a guy from Kannapolis a Ph.D. in education.

I kept reading, hoping that I might come across one that would give me some hint about the information contained within.

"The Effect of Selected Variables on the Educational Orientation of Technical and Vocational Instructors in the North Carolina Community College System." Nope.

"The Effect of Interaction Management Training on Supervisory Behavior Change in the North Carolina Department of Human Resources." Hardly.

"Epitaxial Growth of Thin Films and Quantum Well Structures of Cadmium Telluride by Molecular Beam Epitaxy." Not in a million years.

Wait a minute. Here was one. "Ontogeny and Function of Ultrasonic Vocalization During the Sexual Behavior of Golden Hamsters." I wasn't sure about ontogeny, but I thought I could get a grip on the rest of it. This guy must have studied the love sounds of mating hamsters. But if they were ultrasonic, how did he hear them? Ah, the mysteries of romance and dissertation research.

Another one popped up that I thought I might understand until I thought about it. "Avian Interspecific Utilization of Red-cockaded Woodpecker Cavities." I figured that must have something to do with other birds using the nest holes that woodpeckers carve out of dead trees, but then I got to wondering if it might have something to do with the woodpecker's personal cavities. Does a woodpecker have teeth? Looks like all that battering would shake them out before they had time to get cavities.

The guy who wrote this one surely has a bright future in the computer business, no doubt writing instructional manuals: "Heuristic and Optimal Assignments of Redundant Software Versions and Processors in Fault-tolerant Computer Systems for Maximum Reliability."

Gary Hart might have profited from reading this dissertation that earned a Ph.D in psychology for one of his fellow Colorado residents: "The Effects of Local Exertion and Anticipation on the Performance of a Discrete Skill."

This one caused my hypochondria to perk up: "Dispersal

and Host Preference of Woodland Sharpnosed Leafhoppers, *Scaphytopius magdalensis* (Provancher) and *S. verecundus* (Van Duzee) in Relation to Spread of Blueberry Stunt Disease." What are the symptoms of blueberry stunt disease? Does it make you want to coat yourself in blueberry jam and turn flips off buildings? I think I may have been bitten by a sharpnosed leafhopper just the other day.

Several of these dissertations dealt with food. I was almost certain that I understood what a Kansas woman did to write her dissertation titled "The Effect of Grind, Salt Concentration and Sucrose Concentration on the Flavor and Texture of Peanut Butter." Surely she ground peanuts, added salt and sugar in different amounts and tasted it. But, pray tell, what did this guy from Taiwan do to write "Flavor Components and Phospholipid Changes Associated with the Development of Oxidized Off Flavors in Cooked Turkey Rolls"? By the way, ever tasted a turkey roll with *on* flavors?

Certainly the most useful of this vast batch of dissertations must be this one: "Factors Governing Local Necking in A1 Sheet and Associated Dislocation." I hope that it is published in some popular forum because anybody necking in top-quality sheets ought to know just how far they can go without dislocating any joints.

I Read It In The Newspaper

What Carolinians Fear Most

Sometimes you read the dadgumedest things in the newspaper.

Just the other day, for instance, a story from Paris caught my eye. It was about a survey that had been done in France. A thousand people had been asked what they feared most.

Now I would have thought that such things as dying, being crippled, getting old might have headed the list. Boy, was I wrong.

The thing that French people fear most, according to the survey, was spending a night alone in a country house with a big crawling spider. That was the biggest fear of a full third of the people interviewed.

The second largest number of people, 22 percent, said they were most afraid of being on a mountain or a high statue.

A high statue?

What do French people do on statues anyway? Come to think of it, maybe I don't want to know that.

Anyway, I was beginning to think that maybe the French were more than a little strange. Then I decided to do a survey on the same question right here in North Carolina, and I've had to conclude that the French are no stranger than the rest of us.

For example, 67 percent of women interviewed in Greensboro reported that their biggest fear was of spending a night alone in a country house with a big crawling thing – and discovering that it was Jim Jenkins. Another 12 percent said they would be more afraid of spending a night in Richard Petty's hat.

Twenty-two percent of Piedmont residents said their biggest fear was of being on a high sign with Bob Dunn.

On the other hand, 100 percent of haggard men on Hamburger Square reported being most afraid of not being high on anything.

Of Channel 8 viewers questioned, 17 percent said their greatest fear was of waking up one morning with Frank Deal's hair, while 83 percent said they most feared having to endure more than five of Frank's jokes in a single week.

An amazing 97 percent of Charlotte residents said their biggest fear was of being run over by a freight train hauling Tammy Bakker's mascara to the PTL Club.

In Greensboro, 26 percent of those interviewed said their biggest fear was that the city would rezone their graveyard plots for fast food restaurants.

Yuppies, by a remarkable 72 percent, said their biggest fear was a shortage of alligator emblems. Another 26 percent said they were more scared by nightmares in which Perrier's wells run dry. The remaining 2 percent were most frightened by going to a new Greensboro restaurant not decorated in the color mauve.

Eighty-four percent of residents in exclusive Irving Park were most afraid of being excluded from Martha Long's society column, but 33 percent of motorcycle gang members were most afraid of being mentioned in it.

In the 6th Congressional District, 12 percent of respondents reported being fearful of snagging Congressman Howard Coble by the eyebrows in their Velcro watch bands.

Randolph County zookeepers were unanimous in proclaiming their biggest fear: administering an enema to a rhinoceros without benefit of hip boots.

One patron of a downtown Greensboro watering hole, who has reported encounters with rhinoceroses, elephants and giant crawly creatures on more than one occasion, said he was not as afraid of those as he was of seeing a pregnant woman tap dancing on the bar while singing "Sweet Thang."

Here's a really weird one. Three groggy Greensboro men, who asked that their identities not be revealed, said they were most afraid of being robbed by a-knock-out kissing bandit in Atlantic City.

Ninety-one percent of Greensboro Jaycees said their biggest fear was of losing a Jim Melvin personality contest, but 74 percent of all respondents said their biggest fear was of winning one.

A minuscule 0.00001 percent of born-again Christians reported being most afraid that Jerry Falwell would not accept their cash donations.

Of Carolina alumnae, 76 percent were most frightened of discovering that Dean Smith was not the author of the Ten Commandments.

And a full 100 percent of *Greensboro News & Record* feature columnists said their biggest fear was of beginning an exercise program and not being allowed to write about it.

Our Favorite Fantasies

Sometimes I wonder about the American people.

Take this survey that came out the other day. Some advertising agency wanted to know what the buying public is really like so it commissioned a survey. The way it was reported, I can't say I really understand the results, the percentages and whatnot, but I believe I got the general drift of it.

One thing the survey wanted to find out about was fantasy activities. If you could do anything what would you do?

Guess what was on the top of the list for men. By a big percentage, too.

Getting stranded on a tropical island with the Dallas Cowboys cheerleaders? Being kidnapped by a bunch of ravenous bunnies and held captive at the Playboy Mansion? Sailing around the world with Cybill Shepherd? Climbing Mount Everest with Cybill Shepherd? Being the first man to land on Mars and finding Cybill Shepherd waiting for you?

No. No. No. No. And guess again.

Try going on safari in Africa and shooting some defenseless animal. That was it. On my list, going on safari would come in somewhere just below attending the International Tiddlywink Federation championships.

For women, gambling at Monte Carlo was at the top of the list. Admittedly, that's a notch above shooting a gnu, but is it the thing you would rather do more than anything else? It is a rather sedate and snooty place, after all, and you'd have to get all gussied up. They won't let you wear jeans in those casinos, I'm told. And while gambling has a certain excitement about it, more often than not it results in losing, which in the end, is not exactly an enjoyable experience.

Obviously, the people who responded to this survey didn't put much thought into their answers.

Second on the women's list, for example, was having dinner at the White House, something else that never has entered my mind. I'd be too concerned about using the wrong fork or dumping the mousse into my lap or saying the wrong thing to take any real pleasure out of it. Give me a pizza at home and an old Jimmy Stewart movie on the TV over dinner at the White House anytime. That way, at least, I'd be in the presence of a good actor.

Third on the women's list, and second on the men's, was going to China. Now I'd like to visit China myself. In my book, it ranks far above places like Bulgaria, Iran and Libya as a spot to see. But think about it. China is rather drab and regimented. Not exactly a fun spot. What happened to the romance of the South Seas, the excitement of Rio, the glamor of Paris? Give me any of those before an evening with the commissar of the Ding Po rice co-operative.

Third on the men's list, believe it or not, was camping in the wilderness. I mean, camping has its charms, but if you could do anything you wanted, you'd put getting mosquito bitten, eating out of cans, sleeping on the ground and bathing in cold streams in the top three? Come on now.

I don't know, though. Another question was about what gives us the most pleasure. Eating? Sex? Cuddling and giggling? Laughing? Reading? Golf? Going out to the old ball park? Watching children grow?

Not even in the running. None of them.

The thing that gives Americans the most pleasure, by a whopping 68%, is watching TV. That's what I said. *Watching TV*.

Is that sad, or what? The thing that gives us the most pleasure didn't even exist 60 years ago. Makes you wonder what people used to do for fun, doesn't it?

The only hope in this whole thing lies in the question about the qualities we find most appealing in the opposite sex. Here, at least, you find the answers that you expect. The old standbys. Warmth, sense of humor, intelligence, honesty are

117

far more important, we say, than great bodies and wealth.

Yeah, and I can't wait to come back from my safari and have dinner at the White House.

All lies, of course, as any poor, warm, funny, intelligent and honest person with a less than perfect body surely will attest.

If we're still lying about that to survey takers, maybe we're lying about everything else, too.

Let's hope so. It may be the only hope we've got.

Baptists in Sin City

Sometimes the news is so overwhelming that it is difficult to get a handle on it and grasp just what it means.

Imagine my surprise when I read that the Southern Baptist Convention was going to hold its annual meeting in, of all places, Las Vegas.

The thought of 25,000 Bible-toting Baptists invading the famous Strip is, well, it's nearly mind-boggling.

Common sense would tell you that the Baptists would pick almost any other place. I mean, they're against gambling, so surely they have no use for the casinos. They're against drinking, so out go the bars and most of the restaurants. They don't approve of dancing or excessive exposure of skin, so that eliminates the big showrooms. They certainly want nothing to do with dirty jokes or foul language, so strike the lounges and small showrooms, too.

Did they pick Las Vegas so they can try to save it from itself?

Maybe the bigger question is why Las Vegas invited the Baptists.

Normally, Las Vegas hotels go to great expense and effort to fill their rooms with gamblers who will pack their casinos, bars and showrooms and be loose with their money.

Wouldn't hotels filled with Baptists face empty casinos, empty bars, empty showrooms and empty tills?

And Baptists aren't exactly known for being extravagant with their money. Aren't they likely just to take advantage of the 49¢ breakfasts and $4.99 prime rib dinners offered by hotel restaurants as loss leaders and never even drop a quarter in a slot machine?

Is that why the Baptists picked Las Vegas? Or did they just want to test themselves in the face of so many worldly temptations?

Is Las Vegas simply gambling that they'll lose that struggle?

Of course, it may just be that Las Vegas wants the Baptists because it is a city of spectacle. Las Vegas always stages the most extravagant shows, the biggest boxing matches, the most difficult and dangerous daredevil stunts. Maybe Las Vegas wants the Baptists because it knows what a cat fight the annual convention usually turns out to be.

But on to more difficult-to-comprehend news.

On the same day that I read that the Baptists would be invading Las Vegas, I also learned that scientists have discovered something that most men have long suspected: women's brains are structured differently than men's.

Will this lead at last to answers to those eternal questions: why so many women spend so much time shopping and why women can only go to public rest rooms in groups?

The next day's newspaper brought the unsurprising news that North Carolina's biggest show, the General Assembly of clowns and buffoons now performing in Raleigh, continues to devote itself to frivolities.

When a vote arose in the Senate to ban bumper stickers considered to be obscene, five members who are lawyers warned that the law would be a patent violation of the First Amendment.

"Whether it's constitutional or not, you've got to look at it as what is right or what is wrong," said the bill's sponsor, Sen. Aaron Plyer of Union County.

Whereupon the Senate voted overwhelmingly that the Constitution is wrong when it comes to trifling matters such as free speech.

Finally, in coming to grips with news that's difficult to grapple with, I offer this little item from *USA TODAY*:

> LOS ANGELES – Seven people, including a 350-pound professional female wrestler known as 'Mount Fuji,' were

charged with throwing rocks and bottles at sheriff's deputies in a melee at a bridal shower. Fifteen officers were injured; two were knocked unconscious.

Here is a perfect example of a news story that tells you everything except what you want to know. Whose bridal shower was this? Was it Mt. Fuji's? Was it she who erupted? What set her off? Who called the cops?

What does all of this mean? Sometimes the news is just too overwhelming to understand.

Sexy Sweat

I came across an item this week that is a near perfect example of what is wrong with journalism today.

The new rules in journalism seem to be: 1) Never write a story if you can make a chart instead. 2) If you're forced to write something, pick a sexy topic and condense it until it says practically nothing and drives the reader crazy with unanswered questions.

The primary practitioner of this type of journalism is *USA TODAY*. So it should come as no surprise that this is where I came upon the above-mentioned item. I offer it here in its entirety.

> **SEXY SWEAT**
>
> The scent of a woman's underarm works "somewhat like an aphrodisiac," according to a team of the Athena Institute for Women's Wellness Research in Haverford, Pa. The researchers collected sweat from assorted donors underarms and froze it. A year later, the thawed sweat was rubbed on the upper lips of 11 women three times weekly. During this time, sexual activity heightened, according to the research published in *Physician's Weekly*.

Catches your attention, right?

But what does it actually tell you? Do you really know more than you did before you read it? Or are you, like me, crying out for answers to all the questions left begging?

Let's start with some of the obvious questions. Just what

is the Athena Institute and why is it so concerned with underarm odor to begin with?

How did this research come about? Was a male director of this outfit at a meeting when an attractive woman beside him raised her hand to ask a question and he suddenly found himself overwhelmed with desire by her underarm stains? Did he immediately spirit her off to a lab to begin this project? If this was indeed how it happened, would the world have had benefit of this research if the woman beside him had weighed 400 pounds and looked like Ernest Borgnine?

But let's get to technical questions. Is underarm sweat any different than, say, elbow sweat or knee sweat? Surely it must be, or just any old sweat would have been used. What makes it different?

How, I wonder, was this sweat collected and in what quantity? Were the donors ticklish about giving it?

Why was the sweat frozen? And why for a year? Does freezing it somehow increase its potency? Would freezing it for two years make it twice as strong?

The report says that after a year the sweat was thawed and rubbed on the upper lips of 11 women three times weekly. Who were these women? Were they the original donors of the sweat? Was their own sweat rubbed on their lips, or was it somebody else's sweat? If it was somebody else's sweat, how much did they have to pay these women to get them to allow that?

Speaking of that, why was it rubbed only on the upper lip, as opposed to, say, the wrists and behind the ears, where perfume is commonly dabbed or sprayed? Was the idea to put it under the woman's nose to see if it excited her? If so, shouldn't male underarm sweat have been used?

The report doesn't say how long this research went on, but it does note that during this time sexual activity "heightened."

For whom? The women themselves? The men they encountered? Everybody within a five-mile radius? Did these women stir passions to the extent that they left a wake of lovemaking wherever they went?

What exactly does "heightened" mean anyway? Did sex

occur more frequently? Last longer? Seem better? Occur only while wearing platform shoes? Does this whole thing make any sense at all? I mean, if you suspected that female underarm sweat was an aphrodisiac, why go through all the rigmarole of collecting it, freezing it, rubbing it on lips a year later, when you could just let a group of women run around until they worked up a good sweat and have them go flapping their arms at their lovers or potential lovers and see what happened?

Must've been some big government grant involved to cause this institute to drag it out so long and make such a production of it.

Of course, *USA TODAY* probably wouldn't see fit to tell us about that. Not sexy enough, I'm sure.

Adrift in the Abdominal Sea

Have you noticed how helpful the media have been lately? I'm talking specifically about newspapers and TV. They are going to extra effort to explain things that they apparently consider to be too complicated or obscure for us to understand.

All you had to do to appreciate this in the past few days was turn on the TV. You wouldn't have had to wait long for a diagram of a prostate gland to flash onto the screen.

It wasn't enough for the TV reporters to tell us that President Reagan was having a minor operation to make his trips to the bathroom a little easier. They also felt a need to explain the intricate mechanics of the prostate and its relation to other nearby organs.

At times, it was almost like a travelogue of the lower intestinal region. "While not as popular as the beautiful beaches of the isles of Langerhans, which lie due north, the prostate has its own exotic appeal. One word of caution if you plan to vacation here, however: don't drink the water."

TV wasn't alone in this. Tuesday this newspaper also had a story about the prostate. It quoted one Nicholas Constantinople (not Istanbul), a Washington urologist, as saying, "A surprising number of men don't know what their prostate is for or where it is."

While I'll have to admit that I was never really sure what a prostate was for, I did have an idea of its general vicinity thanks to several doctors over the years who have gotten apologetic looks on their faces, pulled on rubber gloves and asked me to bend over so that they could make certain that my prostate had not broken anchor and been set adrift in the Great Abdominal Sea.

This story went on to report that after age 40 the prostate begins to swell because of a condition called benign prostatic hypertrophy, which isn't nearly as bad as it sounds, the major complication from it being that it could make your trips to the bathroom difficult and unpleasant, as it did for the president. It can be easily corrected with a surgical procedure that requires no incision.

Helpfully, the story went on to describe this remarkable procedure in such elaborate and technical detail that I hesitate to repeat it here. Let's say that if it were a trip, it would be a spelunking adventure with some very tight squeezes in a fragile and sensitive environment. It surely was enough to cause me, age 46, to cringe in sympathy for the president.

The prostate was not the only area in which the paper tried to be helpful Tuesday.

While the president was undergoing a personal gouging, he was submitting us to one of another sort: His trillion-dollar budget. That news was on the front page. Inside, helpfully, was another story explaining just how much a trillion dollars is in terms we all can grasp.

For example, it pointed out that if somebody paid you a dollar a word to read every word in the *Washington Post*, you'd be reading the entire *Washington Post* every day for 34,247 years before you earned a trillion dollars. Sounds like a Jesse Helms vision of purgatory, wouldn't you say?

To bring matters into even better perspective, the story noted that if somebody handed you a $100 bill every second until you had a trillion dollars, it would take you 317 years to accumulate it all. What it didn't say was that well before you reached the third century you'd likely not only be a little frayed from sitting up accepting all of those $100 bills, you'd probably be frantic with concern about where you were going to store them. I mean, how much room would it take? The Astrodome? And once you got it all, would you feel like spending it? The story, unfortunately, didn't say.

A little helpful advice: If somebody offers you a trillion dollars just to sit there and accept it at $100 a second, turn it down. Don't be a sucker.

One disturbing thing about Tuesday's paper was that there was no helpful explanatory story to put into perspective the front-page news that astronomers think they just observed the birth of a new galaxy, which actually happened 12 billion light years ago. That means that this galaxy is 71 billion trillion miles from earth.

Now if you wanted to go to this galaxy and you decided to leave a trail of $100 bills to mark your path, how many should you take with you? How big a spaceship would you need? And if you wanted to read every word in the *Washington Post* every day on your trip, how long a subscription should you sign up for? Should you invite Jesse Helms to go with you?

I searched the paper through for answers to these questions without finding them.

No matter how helpful the media try to be, somehow it just never seems to be quite helpful enough, does it?

I Wuv U

Valentine's Day always gets off to a slow start with me, because I end up spending three times as long with the newspaper as usual.

That, of course, is because of the Valentine Love Lines in the classified pages.

Every year, I swear I'm not going to do it. I'm not going to get suckered in and waste an hour reading other people's silly valentine messages.

Then I open up the paper to that double page spread with those little red hearts and before I realize it, I'm doing it again.

The problem, see, is that I decide to take one little peek to find out if anybody put one in for me. So I glance over to the H's to see if there are any messages for Hunk, and next thing I know I'm hooked.

I'm sad to report that I didn't have one again this year. There was one to Hunk-A-Bunk, but it was from another Hunk and was a sad one about a year having passed and missing you and maybe there's a chance still and all that stuff.

Anyway, after that I got to jumping around reading different ones, and then I said what the heck, I may as well just start at the top and go all the way through, the way I do every year.

I admit it can be a bit of an ordeal, because most of these things are pretty bland, or just nonsensical (roses-are-red-violets-are-blue), but there are some awfully intriguing ones too. I can't help but wonder about the relationships of a lot of the people who appear in these messages.

What do you suppose J means when she tells Desperado to "come down from your fences and let somebody love you before it's too late"? Is he a fence builder, a fence sitter, or both? Whatever, it sounds as if J may be getting fed up.

Why does Barbara feel the need to tell Dexter "I'm not crazy"?

And what about Diane (55), who sent Bill (44) this mysterious message: "143 Forever." Is this older woman, younger man? Are they math teachers or something? What is all this number business anyway? How could you be satisfied with 143 forever when so many higher numbers are available?

Speaking of contentment, consider the relationship of Jeff S. and Beth S. Jeff is the "best-looking blue-eyed blonde-headed mechanic" Beth knows. She is his "eternal flashlight holder." I'll bet Jeff never has to worry about buying flowers or candy or any of that other romantic folderol. "Hand me that sparkplug wrench," is all he has to say and Beth, no doubt, is in heaven.

I'm dying to know what's going on in this one. It's from Ben to Robin. "Can't fight this feeling anymore! Do you think Ruth would approve?" Wanna make a guess whether Ruth does or not?

Nobody has to guess that fishing plays a big part in the love life of Wayne, who was the prize catch of the Bream Reaper. Or that love must be a gamble to Marg, who was warned by Rascal not to "crap out the hard way this Valentine's."

But what about Willie, the Window Woman, and Len, the Window Man? Are they voyeurs? Do they play out peeping fantasies? Have they ever been arrested?

And what about B who thanked Dink for the "5th best year of my life"? How do you rank the years of your life? And isn't it a little less than diplomatic to thank somebody for one that came in only fifth? If I were Dink, I think I'd be wanting to know who gave B the four better years.

If I were the authorities, I think I'd be interested in tracking down and keeping an eye on somebody who calls himself Mr. Goodbar, a blatant candy fetishist who inserted a highly suggestive message that decency won't allow me to reprint addressed to nobody. This, no doubt, is a guy who makes obscene calls to candy stores and probably knows 101 exotic uses for M&Ms.

As usual, this year's valentine love lines were crowded with goofy nicknames – Mushmouf and Punkinpuss, Peanut Butter and Jelly, Dear Dog and Your Wog, Huncheon and Boo Boo Don, Lumpy and Packy, Miss Piggy and Baby Ham, Spade and Billygoat, Pooker and Cooter, Peety and Poody – but some of these nicknames are getting a little out of hand.

I mean, I don't believe I'd allow anybody to call me Goo Goo Head, not even somebody called Goochins. And if my wife put a valentine's message in the paper addressed to Speedy, I think I'd have a word or two with her about it.

It's an amazement to me that somebody called Poot Baby could have a friend, much less a lover expressing undying affection, but I guess there's somebody for everybody, no matter their particular problems. At first, I thought that message might be addressed to a colleague who sits near me, but I don't think she knows anybody named Smookie.

If I were known as Spiderman, I don't believe I'd be comfortable with a lover or a mate who calls herself Black Widow. And if I were called Stinker Dinker, I don't believe I'd be placing any public ads.

Some pet names tell whole stories. Such as Aardvark Nose and Ferret Face. Aren't you happy they found each other? When "Doctor" David and "Nurse" Gail get together, is there any doubt about the games they play?

Should Butterfly really be with Caterpillar? I mean, isn't one likely to be just a little too mature for the other.

One thing I can't help wonder about is Poochie's love life with Ninja Man: "I don't mind the war wounds," she says. From her hospital bed?

Shouldn't Poochie maybe be with Bad Dog, who got this message from Binky: "Life without you was like the inside of Smidgeon's head. Empty."

Who is poor empty-headed Smidgeon? And shouldn't he maybe be with Puddinhead, who claims to love Sexy Bottomed Man?

Has Sexy Man really bottomed? Should Ninja Man have anybody at all?

Ah, the wonders that Love Lines inspire are many indeed.

Can you help but wonder if Bob really has any idea what ILYIHBBMTT means?

What could Cop mean in sending this News Release to Dawne: "The Space Ship HS has crashed in deep water. Please send Tang for thirsty astronaut."

What was the "lip slip" for which Barrie is thanking Karen? Why is Dez congratulating Pam on her DST? Why is Laura telling Reid: "Fruit Loops, picnics & 100 pounds of clay."

What is Ronie asking for in telling Best Friend to "make the car go BOOM?" Should the police be looking into that?

Whatever could have been the big surprise that Andrea had for Ivory on Valentine's Night?

And what did Rhonda really mean in telling Lyle that she loved him "more than an intake manifold?"

I'm sure we'll never know the answers to all these mysteries, but they help to make Valentine's Day a lot more interesting, don't they?

It is a nice feeling to be immersed in so much love. And this year there seemed to be more than ever.

This year's Love Lines seemed simpler, more sentimental, less risque than in year's past. Maybe, I thought, we really have entered a kinder, gentler time.

Then I came upon the message that Lisa sent to Dale: "Mr. 'Early.' I hope your Valentine's Day is miserable & the FBI, CIA & DEA comes to get you!"

The one LaVerne sent to her husband, David, was tempered with love but still not the kind of thing you'd want to get up and read with your morning cup of coffee: "You make me sick, but I love you very much."

Eddie must not have been on his best behavior lately either, but Dianna sounds forgiving: "Roses are red, violets are blue," she wrote. "You sure are MOODY & I love you."

Some of the Love Lines, however, seemed tinged with sadness, placed by people begging forgiveness or longing for lost love. Something about a few also led me to believe that they likely were exercises in futility.

Such as this one to Sarah from Matt: "Roses are red,

violets are blue, sure I asked your sister on a date but I still want to go with you. Call me sometime." Don't you expect old Matt will be waiting a while on that call?

And, no doubt, Chuck didn't do himself any favors when he addressed this to Lori: "Roses are pink, carnations are yellow. I'm bound and determined to be your only fellow. But if you have doubts that will last another day, just stop and remember the guy who paid your way."

Yeah, pal, and you'll probably be paying for ads like this for a long time too.

One more thing. A personal note to Kenneth, who bought a big valentine to Robin, My Love. A grown man doesn't say "I wuv you" even in private, much less in public print.

Preachers, Parties
and Other Particulars

Won't You Come Home, Jim Bakker

Here's one news story you may have missed during all the hullabaloo about the Jim Bakker-PTL affair:

WASHINGTON – A columnists' group is urging its members to join in a national prayer vigil to have Jim Bakker reinstated as leader of the PTL Club.

"Let's face it," said Cadge Wattukan, columnist for the Loon Lake, Minn., *Hooter* and president of Columnists Aligned for Religious Philandering (CARP). "We are distraught. We are devastated. Jim Bakker's resignation was the worst blow to column writing since Elizabeth Taylor slimmed down."

In a press conference at the National Press Club, Wattukan noted that for five years straight, America's columnists have voted Jim and Tammy Bakker their Fun Couple of the Year and devoted more space to them than to any other topic.

"In some cases," said Wattukan, "the Bakkers and PTL have accounted for as much as 10 percent of total output."

Wattukan said that columnists all over the country had been calling him in despair and desperation since Bakker's resignation.

"We fear that without Jim and Tammy at the helm, PTL could collapse," Wattukan said, "and that would put a serious strain on some of our members to come up with enough material to fill their columns. Heaven knows, we have a hard enough time as it is."

The consensus among columnists, said Wattukan, was that some unified action should be taken to get Bakker's job back.

"We think that Bakker's indiscretions were merely peccadillos and not serious enough to deprive him of the empire he built through years of back-breaking begging and groveling," Wattukan said. "Basically, our members feel that he has not done anything that we might not have done ourselves if only we had the opportunity to meet that type of church secretary."

Wattukan noted that the prayer vigil was but one response to the crisis planned by his organization. Members of the columnist group were also being asked to volunteer personal services to Jim and Tammy as a means of enticing them back, he said.

"Some, for example, have offered to polish the gold plumbing in their Rolls Royce," he said. "Others, and there are quite a few of these, have said they would be glad to come in once a week to shine the floor-to-ceiling mirrors in the bedroom of Bakker's Florida beach condominium now that they know they are being put to purposes other than just allowing God to see the ocean from any point in the room, as Bakker previously stated."

Wattukan said he hoped morning radio disc jockeys and editorial cartoonists, who also have benefited greatly from the Bakkers' activities, would join the columnists in their vigil and campaign.

After the press conference, Wattukan joined other columnists in the Press Club bar, where they vowed to pray until Bakker was reinstated – or somebody bought them a round of drinks.

In a random sampling taken after the press conference, columnists and disc jockeys pronounced themselves strongly in favor of the effort.

"If all the ink I've gotten out of Jim and Tammy could be turned into eyeliner, I'm sure it would supply Tammy for nearly a week," said Scuz Andmore of the Appleton, Wisc., *Appeal*, who voiced strong support. "I don't know how I'll be able to get along without them."

A Greensboro, N.C., columnist, who was ashamed to be identified, promised to fast on nothing more than Lexington barbecue, Moon Pies, Cheerwine and Krystal burgers – if he could get them – until the Bakkers return.

"Count me in!" said Billy Bob Beanhead, morning man for WUPP-FM Radio in Spartanburg, S.C. Beanhead claims to be the first DJ to nickname PTL the Pass The Loot Club. "Bakker's got to come back because I've got this great idea. See, I'm going to call it Pass The Lust."

Joe Don "Headlock" Grappler, former high school wrestling star and columnist for the Deep Sludge, Miss, *Muckraker*, said that if the Bakkers didn't soon regain control of PTL, "I'm aimin' to put a hurtin' on somebody."

Grappler said he wanted to talk to Bakker about an idea he has for a new venture at Heritage Village, Bakker's religious recreational community near Charlotte, N.C.

"It come to me when I seen Brother Oral Roberts on TV the other night telling how he rassled the devil in his bedroom," Grappler said. "I said to myself, 'Now why should

Brother Oral rassle the devil in the privacy of his bedroom when people would pay good money to see it?' I want Brother Jim to put in a rasslin' arena next to his water park. He could call it Rasslin' For Jesus. He could get Brother Oral to rassle the devil on weekends and during the week he could have mud rasslin' matches between Tammy and Jessica Hahn. I bet Tammy would like that, and it ought to really pull 'em in, praise God!"

"Jim and Tammy who?" said Jim Jenkins, a former columnist turned, heaven forbid, editorial writer. "Do they have anything to do with acid rain or Star Wars?"

Jenkins said that writing a column for more than four years had caused him to undergo a recent religious experience in which the Lord instructed him to ascend into an Ivory Tower to pray and write anonymously about nothing but important subjects until his psyche was cleansed and he had restored some dignity to his family name.

"I'm sorry," he said, "But I just don't have time to be bothered by something like this."

Tricking Brother Oral

Oral Roberts must be really ticked off today.

If not for some meddling dog track owner in Florida, this would have been Brother Oral's first day in heaven.

But instead of strolling the streets of gold sipping milk and honey, or trying out his new wings, he's still stuck in Tulsa, worrying about his income taxes and waiting to hear what new money-raising schemes God has in mind for him.

Brother Oral's ultimatum from God to raise millions or be unceremoniously snatched up to heaven has been overshadowed in recent days by the Jim Bakker debacle, but a lot of unanswered questions linger in its wake nonetheless.

One of them is this: Can the Lord's work be accomplished with tainted money? The source of the $1.3 million that saved Brother Oral's life is, after all, dog tracks, and the source of dog track money is gambling. For as long as I can remember, preachers have told us gambling is a sin. This would seem to have put Brother Oral in an awkward position. A genuine dilemma.

Does he accept the fruits of sin in the Lord's name? Or does he pass it up on moral grounds, fall short of the Lord's demands and get zapped for it?

Which, in heaven's name, is the right course?

Apparently, Brother Oral wasn't as eager to go home to heaven as one might expect a preacher to be. He took the money and opted for Tulsa.

That had to be a hard decision. From what I've heard about the place, offered the choice of a weekend in Tulsa or eternity in the hereafter's other option, some people might seriously consider the latter.

Anyway, this whole business raises several more questions. Did the Lord tell Brother Oral to take that money? Surely on such a big decision as that, Brother Oral wouldn't have acted on his own.

We can only assume that the Lord must've told him that gambling money was all right as long as it is put to such constructive purposes as building prayer towers or sending missionaries to Tanganyika.

What I can't help but wonder is how far the Lord is willing to go on a deal like this. If gambling money is acceptable, how about drug money? Or porno profits? Or Mafia donations?

And if it is indeed OK to take money from such questionable sources, why fool around waiting on the whims of middlemen to provide it?

Why not go directly to the source? Brother Oral's prayer tower would make a fine casino. With a view to boot. He could fill it with slot machines whirling with angels and crosses and other religious symbols – three golden crowns is a jackpot. He could put in whitejack tables.

If that didn't provide sufficient income, with a few connections in Columbia, or an introduction to Larry Flynt, Brother Oral no doubt could get into other lucrative ventures for the Lord.

Better yet, he could just refine his fund-raising techniques with a few minor adjustments All he'd have to do is organize groups of thugs into Goons for God squads and send them out to prowl through retirement centers and nursing homes using strong-arm techniques to take Social Security checks.

But let's assume God would draw the line on this kind of activity. Let's say he tells Brother Oral and all the other TV evangelists he won't condone accepting drug or porno money or robbery receipts no matter how much he'd like to have a new prayer tower or TV station or water park built in his name.

We still are left with the reality of this gambling money that Brother Oral already has taken.

If we assume that the Lord told Brother Oral to take it, then we have to also assume the Lord told this millionaire dog track owner to give it.

If that's true, there seems to be but one obvious conclusion. The Lord must approve of gambling.

That being the case, either the preachers who have been condemning gambling all these years must be wrong, or the Lord has had a recent change of mind.

Incidentally, I wonder if the Lord's been in communication with my friend Coy Privette about this? Brother Coy has been busily organizing against a lottery and a horse racing track in North Carolina in recent months, and it might be embarrassing to him to find out that the Lord is in favor of it.

Of course, the Lord may not appreciate gambling at all. Maybe he was just setting up a real tricky test for Brother Oral.

I've been trying to figure out how Brother Oral figured this thing. If he accepted the money, meeting the Lord's goal, it would seem that he should get some kind of reward. But no, he is punished and made to stay in Tulsa instead of going off to Heaven, the ultimate reward.

If he didn't accept the money, it would appear he might be defying the Lord's demand, yet the punishment for his defiance is a fast trip to Heaven, ultimate reward.

It's all very confusing, but I still can't see why Brother Oral didn't just turn down the offer and go on to Heaven while he had the chance.

He's got to be ticked off at being tricked into staying in Tulsa like that.

Discretion Advised

Readers are advised that discretion should be exercised in reading this column.

Explicit material will be discussed.

Children under 18 should not be allowed beyond this point without adult supervision. Adults with high blood pressure or a history of heart problems might also want to exercise caution, as well as anybody with good taste or an IQ above 60.

If this were TV news, we would play a little bump-and-grind music here and show some lurid pictures of scantily clad women moving suggestively, but this, alas, is not TV, so you will just have to imagine such a scene for yourself. Chances are, the one you imagine will be even better anyway.

If you have not exercised discretion by now, it can be assumed that you are staying tuned for the good stuff, which is, of course, the whole purpose of offering up the titillating information that explicit material is forthcoming.

We are going to get very explicit here, friends, though we can't show you any near nudity or play any get-down music. Those are problems that we are working on overcoming. I mean if a greeting card can play music, why can't a column? And editors are even now meeting about my proposal to develop fold-out centerfolds for this space.

I want to point out here, however, that we are not getting explicit just for explicitness' sake. And neither should it be assumed that we approve of the explicitness about which we are about to be explicit. And this explicitness has nothing at all to do with the fact that this happens to be sweeps weeks in the column writing trade, the time when the National Column Writers Association surveys readers to determine if anybody is reading anything churned out by the poor wretches who have to stoop to this for a living.

I should state that we are only being explicit because this, of course, is an important issue, and the only way that we can deal with it is by being explicit.

I cannot stress enough the seriousness of this issue, and again I apologize for having to be explicit about it, but believe me it is absolutely necessary.

Is the room cleared of children?

Friends, I'm sorry to report that – oh, I'm almost too embarrassed to write this – that we have undergone a...well, I'll just go ahead and say it...a pubic hair violation!

Right here in Greensboro, North Carolina.

I know. You never dreamed you'd live to see this day, did you?

I am not making this up, by the way. I would never make up something this serious. I heard it with my own ears, coming from my very own TV. Right in the middle of the news.

Perhaps your attention, like mine, was caught by a weeklong series of reports on Channel 8's WGHPiedmont News devoted to "uncovering" the topless bars in these parts. Seems the station assigned a crack investigative reporter by the name of Olivia Dorn-Kennedy to look into this situation, and she spent a month or so doing it.

Her major finding, as best I could tell, came Wednesday night. Apparently it is legal to dance topless hereabouts so long as no touching is involved, the dancing does not simulate sexual activity and no genitalia or pubic hair is exposed.

On Wednesday night, Dorn-Kennedy reported she had gone "undercover" to these bars (bar owners take note: She was the one with the big nose and funny glasses, wearing a trench coat and fedora and lugging a TV camera on her shoulder) and had observed a clear pubic hair violation.

I can't tell you the extent of this violation because Dorn-Kennedy, inexplicably, was not explicit about it. We can't be sure whether it was a single hair or a swath, but I could tell that it was a grave matter by the somber expressions on the faces of news anchors Fred Blackman and Cynthia Smoot when

143

they talked with Dorn-Kennedy about it at the conclusion of her report.

Are we in danger? Should the National Guard be alerted?

Unfortunately, Dorn-Kennedy did not deal with these vital questions in the final segment of her report Thursday night. She only showed more scantily clad women moving suggestively.

The public should remain calm, however, as I have decided to go undercover myself to investigate this matter more thoroughly. Stay tuned for my six-part series, "Pubic Hair: Friend or Foe?" Readers are advised to exercise discretion.

Stuff Happens in Florida

I've always liked Florida. I go there at least once a year and try to get back more often if I can. But I'm afraid to go now because of a new law that state enacted last week.

The law seeks to rid Florida's streets and highways of bumper stickers the state deems to be offensive or obscene. According to news reports, these include bumper stickers with messages that contain double-entendres and sexual innuendo.

And the law leaves it to individual police officers to determine just what is offensive or obscene. The driver of the vehicle bearing the offensive sticker can be fined $600 and sent to jail for six months. A second offense causes the penalties to double.

Let's say I drive down to Florida, perfectly innocent, my bumper free of stickers, and I stop at, say, a seafood joint for lunch, and unbeknownst to me, the owner, eager to increase business, slaps a bumper sticker on my car that says "I got crabs at Joe's."

Then I finish my lunch and pull out onto the street and the first thing I see is a blue light behind me, and some cop who has completely misinterpreted the message on my bumper hauls me off to the cooler. Am I going to be crabby about this? You better believe it.

Or consider this. A staid Republican is tooling down I-95 in his new Cadillac on his way to a golfing weekend in Palm Beach. A cop spots his bumper sticker proclaiming his love for his presidential candidate and reads it the wrong way. Is this upright citizen apt to be pleased at the prospect of having an obscenity charge on his record? Not likely.

What if some innocent family man is taking his wife and

kids to the beach at Daytona, his car still bearing on its bumper the evidence of a trip to the mountains near Chattanooga last summer, and some Florida cop sees it and asks himself, "Ruby Falls? For what?" Is this poor guy apt to be yanked out of his car and hauled off to jail while his family is left sitting on the roadside?

One of my favorite bumper stickers is this: "Eschew Obfuscation." What if some cop saw that and thought it sounded dirty, which it does, sort of, now that I think about it. How much trouble would I be in for trying to preach that valuable lesson from my bumper in Florida?

And what about those people who use their bumpers to proclaim their professions? You know, the ones whose cars bear bumper stickers that say, "Engineers do it with precision," "Librarians do it by the book," "Cartoonists do it with animation," "Journalists do it daily," "Truck drivers do it in the road," "Teachers do it with class," "Lawyers do it in their briefs." If some cop should choose to read sexual connotations into these simple statements of professional pride, thousands of innocent tourists could find themselves moldering in Florida jails.

Of course, there isn't likely to be much room in Florida's jails for tourists once the cops begin strict enforcement of this law, because the jails no doubt will be quickly filled with locals whose vehicles sport bumper stickers that say, in essence, that stuff happens, but in a term that is generally considered to be in poor taste and is offensive enough to many people that it surely won't be found in a family newspaper.

I first saw this particular bit of wisdom on a bumper sticker in Florida a couple of years ago, and the last time I was there it seemed to be plastered across half the car bumpers and T-shirts in the state. If somebody who is arrested for displaying one of these particular bumper stickers should choose to fight this law, it could prove to be an interesting case, because the law appears to exempt those bumper stickers that can prove "serious literary, artistic, political or scientific value."

I don't know if this statement could be shown to have political value, since it doesn't pinpoint the source of the stuff that happens. Neither does there appear to be anything artistic about it, but it seems to be a scientific fact that stuff of this nature does indeed happen, and it surely is a serious matter.

I think it also could be shown to have literary value. Philosophy, after all, is a branch of literature, and this is without question a philosophical statement, perhaps the most succinct and apt of our time.

But then, you never know how these things are going to come out. So until some high court rules freedom of bumper is not to be abridged, probably the best thing for visitors to do is to keep out of Florida. And it might even be appropriate to buy a bumper sticker that says, though in far more succinct terms, that if Florida drinks, it's probably through straws.

A High Point in Art

Nincompoopery, I'm happy to see, is still alive and well in High Point, N.C.

I'd been worried about it. High Point long has had a proud history of nincompoopery, especially as regards the arts, but it had been somewhat dormant of late. Now, thank heaven for right-thinking people, it's being revived.

High Point, you may recall, is the city where part of an art show was once shut down as obscene because a painting depicted a seating apparatus common to American bathrooms. It's probably the only city in the world where a plumber's manual could have been considered pornography.

It's also the only city where a theater manager and his projectionist were arrested in mid-show and marched off to jail for showing the movie, *Hawaii.*

Now a city councilman wants it to be the city that banned Puff the Magic Dragon on political grounds.

Councilman Steve Arnold – who previously opposed a holiday honoring Dr. Martin Luther King Jr. on grounds that King associated with communists and fooled around on his wife—objected this week to any appearance in the High Point Theatre by Mary Travers.

I don't know much about Mary Travers except that she is a singer with long, straight blond hair who performed with a group called Peter, Paul and Mary. This group had several hits back in the '60s, including "Puff the Magic Dragon" and "This Land is Your Land." But Arnold says she is "a radical liberal," and, therefore, should not be allowed to perform in High Point Theatre.

Maybe Arnold is right that Mary Travers is a radical

liberal, but does being liberal cause her to sing less sweetly than if she were conservative or moderate? And if being radical is enough to ban someone from singing, is it not likewise enough to ban someone from holding public office?

I mean, is it not just a touch radical to propose that someone meet a political test before being allowed to sing in a public place in a free society?

Be that as it may, considering High Point's history on such matters, you can safely bet that you aren't apt to see Mary Travers singing "Puff the Magic Dragon" at the High Point Theatre, and chances are good that there may be some drastic changes in the type of productions presented at the theater in the future.

Indeed, as a famous senator used to say, I happen to have in my possession a secret document that lists some of the changes that will be forthcoming.

The annual Shakespeare Festival will, of course, be scrapped. Shakespeare's wife, after all, was pregnant before they wed, and he did wear those funny clothes and associate with known actors and poets. Clearly not a man of high moral character.

In the festival's place will be other plays. Among them:

"Another Cinder For Jesus," a drama by Jerry Falwell's Old Time Gospel Players. A professor at a Baptist seminary is tried for heresy for suggesting in a book that moderates be allowed into heaven. The final scene in which the entire cast surrounds the unrepentant professor singing the touching hymn, "We Burn You Out of Love," will not be easily forgotten.

"The Big Blow." Evangelist Pat Robertson plays himself in this dramatic play in which he hides amongst the thousand-dollar suits in his large closet and prevails on God to spare his mansion, limousine and TV studios by redirecting a hurricane into a crowded New Jersey tenement.

"Yassa Massa." The indefatigable Strom Thurmond stars in this heart-warming musical about a South Carolina plantation owner who overcomes the meddling of do-gooders to restore slavery "for the good of the little pickaninnies."

Other shows that will be acceptable at High Point Theatre include:

"The G. Gordon Liddy Show." In this crowd-pleasing audience participation show, people are brought on stage to have their flesh seared with candle flames in tests of will. Roasted rat dinners will be served to those who do not flinch.

"Woman, Know Thy Place" a ballet by the Phyllis Schlafly Dance Ensemble. Schlafly will appear if her husband will let her.

The Jesse Helms Good-Time Goose-Stepping Band in concert. Helms himself will conduct the band's stirring hit, "To The Right March." There will be a special guest appearance by the Dancing Dictators, a South American group that will perform its memorable "Dance on the Graves of Dissidents."

The Sam and David Show. This is expected to be the big hit of the season, and tickets should be bought well in advance. While Sam Currin does a dramatic reading of excerpts of despicable pornography inserted into the Congressional Record by his mentor, Jesse Helms, David Funderburk pantomimes them.

The Was-Adolf-Really-All That-Bad? Barbershop Quartet. This group, formed by members of Ronald Reagan's cabinet, sings nostalgic tunes of the concentration camps.

And finally, the magic of William Rehnquist, in which the Supreme Court chief justice and noted amateur prestidigitator makes the Bill of Rights permanently disappear.

Bring Back Dixie Cups

I came home the other night and found Linda doe-eyed, holding a spoon and looking guilty.

"How ya doin'?" I asked.

"I ate all the froozen glazsha," she said.

She licked the spoon hurriedly, as if she were afraid I might try to grab it from her.

"You did what?"

"I ate all the froozen glazsha."

"You ate all the froozen whazsha?"

"The froozen glazsha," she said, licking the empty spoon again, now looking impish.

"What in the world is froozen glazsha?" I asked.

"You are really out of it, aren't you?" she said. "It's ice cream, of course."

"Well, why didn't you just say you ate all the ice cream?"

"Because this isn't simply ice cream. This is beyond ice cream. If you eat froozen glazsha you do not have to belong to the Junior League. You do not have to live in Irving Park. You do not have to understand the wine list at Madison's. You don't have to drive a Porszha."

"A Porszsha?"

"Yes, a Porszsha."

"I don't know what you're talking about," I said.

"I'm talking about status," she said. "I'm talking about ice cream that causes people to look on in admiration when you push it around in your supermarket cart. I'm talking about ice cream that costs so much that you feel important eating it."

"Costs how much?" I asked suspiciously.

"I don't know. Maybe $47 a pint. Something like that."

"Forty-seven dollars a pint!" I said. "You spent that much for ice cream? Are you crazy?"

"Well, not quite that much," she said. "Anyway, it's cheaper than a Porszsha. And have you checked real estate prices in Irving Park lately?"

"For fifty cents I can get a Dixie Cup," I said. "Perfectly good ice cream. And that is overpriced. When I was a kid, you could get a Dixie Cup for a nickel.

"When you were a kid, you could get a new Cadillac for seven hundred dollars," she said.

I ignored her.

"In a nickel Dixie Cup you not only got ice cream but the lid had a picture of a cowboy movie star on the inside," I said. "I had 23 Gabby Hayeses before I ever got a Bob Steele."

"Who's Bob Steele?"

"Who's Bob Steele!?! Who's Bob Steele!?!" I was incredulous. "And you have the audacity to say *I'm* out of it?"

"Did he eat froozen glazsha?" she asked.

"He never even had a Dixie Cup. They didn't have ice cream in the Old West, silly. All they had was shots of red eye and beef jerky and a few beans."

"I hope he had a Porszsha."

"No, he had a horszsha."

"I think this is getting out of hand," Linda said.

I agreed. The conversation was getting out of hand. But no more so than the ice cream business these days.

Don't get me wrong. I am a big fan of ice cream, but when a single scoop of some ice creams costs enough to buy lunch, and when the price of a pint at the supermarket would feed the average family for a day on less prestigious fare, then you've got to wonder what makes people buy it, right?

You know the ice creams I mean. The ones with the names you can't pronounce or spell. The ones that try to make you think they came from Lapland or some other exotic spot. The ones that cost so much more than any other ice creams.

I mean, how much difference can there be in ice cream?

What is ice cream, after all? Milk, cream, sugar, a little flavoring, some fruit or nuts.

And air. Don't forget air. That is a big factor in commercial ice creams. The more air you put into it, the less you have to put of the other ingredients – and the more profit you make. I'm not sure what this has to do with anything, but I know it because I used to be in the ice cream business myself, and I thought I'd throw it in just to impress.

I'm not sure, though, that my lack of desire to try fancy ice creams made much of an impression on Linda.

"Don't knock it until you've tried it," she said, licking her spoon again.

"The only way I'd put out that kind of money for ice cream," I said, "is if they start putting pictures of Gabby Hayes inside the lid."

Of Boats and Gardens

I have been doing some serious thinking lately about buying a boat.

This is mainly because my friend and fellow columnist, John York of the *Charlotte Observer*, called to tell me he is selling his boat and he thought I might be interested.

It's not a fancy boat, I might mention. Just a little runabout, 12 years old. John knew I would be interested in it, because he and I have talked about boats a lot and he knew that I harbored romantic notions about having one of my own some day.

He didn't know that the real reason I need a boat has nothing to do with romantic notions of speeding across the water to fish in some secluded cove or to lounge in the summer sunshine while the water laps soothingly beneath me.

No, the real reason I need a boat is because I already have a yard and a garden. Maybe I should explain that.

You see, I have this friend by the name of Jim McAllister, a columnist with the Greenville, S.C., *News*. Jim has neither yard, nor garden, nor boat, but he does have a theory about people who have such things.

He thinks that they are basically showoffs, and that's why he's never bothered to have any of those things himself. He discovered that he didn't need to have them because he could get all he needed of them without any of the worries, problems and expenses that attend them.

Take yards. Jim learned the hard way in his youth that having a nice yard requires great expenditures of hard work, sweat and misery and that the payments are never ending. As soon as you finish mowing, trimming and clipping, you just have to do it all over again.

He realized that if he wanted to look at a pretty yard, all he had to do was get in his car and drive around a little and he could see yards to his heart's content. If he wanted to actually get out and walk around in one, or sit in one, that was no problem either.

He discovered that friends who had yards would often invite him over when their yards were at their prettiest, just to show them off. And usually they would even cook him a steak or some other treat on the grill outside so that he would be sure to get a good look at the yard. He would get his fill of good food along with his fill of nice yard, all at no more cost than a few compliments, thus assuring invitations in the future, should he feel the desire to get close to a nice yard again.

The same with gardens. Jim knows what a pitiless and demanding thing a garden can be and long ago rejected the idea of ever having one for those very reasons. But he made the fortunate discovery that people who grow gardens are not only masochists but showoffs as well. They almost always grow far more than they can use and they love to try to impress their friends with their horticultural abilities by sharing their bounty.

Every summer, they give Jim more tomatoes, cucumbers, squash, corn, beans, cantaloupes and other fruit and vege-tables than he can eat, and he never has to turn a hand to grow them. He is careful, however, to compliment the growers on the beauty and tastiness of their crops and their obvious skill at producing them.

Boats might not seem to fall into the same category with gardens and yards, but Jim assures me that they are no different. He likes boats, likes being on the water, and he admits that he has even entertained a few thoughts about having a boat himself.

But he long ago realized the wisdom of the old saying that the two happiest days of a boat owner's life are the day he buys his boat – and the day he sells it. Every time Jim caught himself allowing idle thoughts of buying a boat to wander through his head, he would sit down and add up the number of hours he would be apt to spend on a boat in a year's time, then add up how much it would cost to buy and keep and run a boat for that period, and the cost per hour would always be phenomenal.

"I know all kinds of people who have boats," he said, "and they're always looking for somebody to go riding with them so that they can show off their boats. If I get to feeling that I really need to ride a boat, that I just can't go another hour without getting on a boat, I'll just call one of 'em up and say, 'I was thinking about going fishin',' and they'll say, 'When you want to go?', 'cause they're just waiting for somebody to come along that they can take out and show off that boat. And when I get out there, I always tell 'em, 'This is a real nice boat. You keep it up well, too.' I tell 'em that three or four times, and they can't wait for me to come back and ride on that boat again."

Jim was telling me all of this when I called to ask his advice about buying John's boat. He said he thought I ought to get it. Said he bet it was a really nice boat.

"You'll probably keep it up well, too," he said.

THE Party

I was flabbergasted when I read in Martha Long's society column about THE party of recent history, a fabulous 40th birthday affair for a Greensboro socialite.

How could this be? I wondered. If this party had been just a little more elegant, it would have been a carbon copy of my own 40th birthday party two years ago.

Almost 100 guests also attended our to-do, many in K-mart formality. Upon arrival outside our house, each guest was asked to take an envelope from a tray taken by accident from Big El's Drive-In in Morehead City and still attached to the window of a '73 Ford pickup. Each envelope was personally addressed and contained seat numbers and a coupon good for a free oil change with fill-up at Lube World.

A fleet of Blue Bird cabs were then boarded for the ride to Thomasville's acclaimed Southern restaurant, Wahoo's #1.

Black and white foam rubber dice dangling from rearview mirrors in each cab set an immediate festive mood, aided in no small measure by the fully stocked ice chests in each trunk. On the way, the drivers passed out cellophane sacks of fried pork rinds and Cheez Doodles, the fat ones, along with pate of pickled pigs' feet on Ritz crackers.

In Thomasville, the path from cab to restaurant entrance was lined with some of Thomasville's brightest luminaries, including Frog from the pool room, Smiley, the sign painter, and Slimy, the snowball man.

Inside, all eyes lighted up at the sight. Tables with Formica tops were supposed to have been decorated by topiary trees, but Thomasville's top topiatrist was unavailable due to a personal problem involving a chicken, a massage parlor and a bad check, and we had to settle, alas, for other centerpieces.

Nevertheless, the guests all agreed that the perpetual motion stick birds bobbing into glasses of water were lovely, as were the streamers of kudzu cascading Maypole-style from the ceiling and adorned with gaily colored lights on loan from a Good Neighbor Sam camping group.

At each place, a box, wrapped and tied in yellow, contained a package of Doan's Little Pills with the new tamperproof seal and inscribed with the date past which they shouldn't be taken.

As guests found their places, a Wurlitzer jukebox – once played by Rufus Edmisten – struck up "Honky Tonk Angel" from the corner, and if I remember correctly, Linda placed a plate of mashed potatoes, or a facsimile thereof, atop my head, and from then until the last cab returned home, the small dance floor was a mess. Except for an hour and a half during which Jim Jenkins did an amusing demonstration with a ketchup bottle, some guests also danced.

But certainly not during supper. My, what a meal!

If you know your Southern, you'll know what I mean, and if you don't then you don't know good eatin'.

The white wine accompanying the pawpaw soup was a Duplin County Scuppernong, 1980, which went equally well with the potted meat Armour Star. Pamplemoose snowballs, handscraped by Slimy, refreshed the palate for the main course, Supreme de Jerryus country style steakus, served with a sweetened iced tea, Luzianne, 1981. The salad course, coleus slawus, followed, prompting some guests to wonder why it arrived so late. The dessert, Poire Boiye's banana pudding, added clout to the gastronomical merger.

At the top of the printed menus was the date and at the bottom an ad for Honest John's Used Cars.

Among the guests, Kay Hall looked especially fetching in her purple tap shoes and did several nice numbers accompanying herself on kazoo, although nobody paid much attention. Midway through the evening Big Af passed out a batch of painters hats from his Williamsburg Paint and Decorating Center, and everybody who got one asked what it was for.

Wurlitzer music is known in honky-tonk social circles all over the nation, and Harriet Lee, dancing with husband Bill, loved every minute of it – she said it took her back to Martinsville.

Gov. Jim Hunt was seen spraying his hair in the rest room, and Nat Walker, the dapper PR-man for R.J. Reynolds, interrupted a tour with country music stars Slim Whitman and Roy Drusky and flew in from Bloomington, Ind., to pass out Pride In Tobacco bumper stickers.

As the guests reluctantly reloaded the cabs for the trip home, a liqueur of gin and Cheerwine was served in hollowed-out Mallo Cups, and each guest was offered a hygienically wrapped mint-flavored tooth pick.

Many guests proclaimed that this party was their peak personal experience. Stan Swofford said it would have been his, if not for an episode in an alley in Saigon in 1967.

You must be wondering why you didn't read about such an elegant party as this in Martha Long's column two years ago. Well, we didn't invite Martha because we thought it would be unfair to ask her to come and not write about it. We didn't want to be gauche and flaunt such an affair.

But now I wish we'd invited her. I'm sure she would've had a marvelous time.

The Agony of Victory

Pulling for the Brewers

My friend was flabbergasted when she found out I was indifferent to the World Series.

"You mean you're not pulling for the Brewers?" she said. "Everybody should be pulling for the Brewers."

"Why should I be pulling for the Brewers?" I said.

"Harvey Kuenn. That's why. He's had two heart attacks or two cardiac surgeries or something like that. And he's got a wooden leg. I think it's his right leg, or maybe it's his left leg."

"You mean the Brewers have got a player with a wooden leg?" I said. "How does he run?"

"He's not a player. He's the manager. Don't you know anything?"

I admitted that when it comes to baseball, I don't know much. "How did he lose his leg?" I asked.

"He'd been on the golf course, I think. Anyway, he found out he was going to have to have that done, because of his circulation or something. His wife tells this nice little story about it.

"I can't remember whether his wife's name is Harriet or Henrietta or Estelle, but it's one of those types of names, and she says when he found out he was going to have to have his leg taken off, he said, 'Why me?' But before anybody could even answer he said, 'That's the dumbest question I ever asked in my life.' And then he said, 'Let's get on with it. I want to get on the golf course.'

"That's just his attitude about life, and that's what I like about him. That's not all I like about him. I like three more things about him. You want to know what they are?"

"Sure."

163

"Well, he chews the biggest wad of tobacco you have ever seen. I mean, you wouldn't believe . . . he must have a whole pack in his mouth at one time. His jaw goes out like 10 bees stung him, but he can talk with all that tobacco in his mouth and no juice even runs out the side. I don't know whether he swallows the juice or spits it out, but none of it ever runs out, which is amazing to me.

"The second thing I like about him, besides his illness and his tobacco, is that he and his wife, Eloise, or Harriet, or Henrietta, they live in Milwaukee...or Detroit one. They wouldn't live in Detroit, would they? Anyway, they run a bar and they live behind the bar. That's where they live. They don't live in some mansion just because he's a big baseball manager. They live behind the bar. I just think that's wonderful. They're so neat. I just love that.

"And the third thing, when he came to that team, he told 'em he doesn't cotton much to meetings and he doesn't like to walk out to the mound. You know why they walk out to the mound, don't you?"

"Not exactly," I said.

"They go to try to settle the pitcher down and a lot of it's show and stuff, but when he walks out there, he means business. He's just no nonsense. He wades right through the garbage and gets to the heart of the matter. No fluff for Harvey Kuenn."

"Really sounds like he's something," I said.

"Well, you should pull for the Brewers, because somebody in that kind of health, he can kick off any time, and wouldn't it be great if they could win a World Series so if he has to kick off, he'd have won a World Series? It would have to make it not hurt quite as much to kick off if you'd won a World Series."

"I suppose so," I said.

"But that's not the only reason you should pull for the Brewers. You should pull for 'em because that Gorman Thomas – he's that guy with the long, bunched-out sideburns; he's got a big mustache and a pot belly; you can tell he drinks a beer, in other words – he's right at the top of the home run hitters, but the reason you should pull for him is because he went to James Island High School in Charleston. That's where I went to high school.

"And he went to high school with my brother. He was just an ol' – I hate to use the word hoodlum, that doesn't sound right, but that's what he was, just a good ol' boy kind of hoodlum, and who would've ever thought when ol' Gorman Thomas got out of James Island High School that he would've been a key person in the World Series?

"But that's what he is. Nobody at James Island High School ever amounted to anything like that. He's the most famous person who ever came out of James Island High School.

"I don't guess that everybody would care that he went to James Island, but everybody ought to care about what they did to that Ladd fellow, that probation officer."

"Probation officer?" I said. "What did they do to him?"

"Didn't you see it? They robbed him. They put him in to pitch because that Rollie Fingers is hurt and couldn't. Isn't that a great name for a pitcher, Rollie Fingers? He's got an ol' timey mustache that curls up on the edges and looks real hard. Gosh, I couldn't stand to kiss him. I don't know how anybody kisses anybody like that.

"Anyway, they put in that probation officer. He wears a 15 and a half shoe. *A 15 and a half shoe!* That's not the reason you should pull for him, because he wears a 15 and a half shoe. You should pull for him because he's a nice guy and he's funny, and they put him in and he threw that strike that they called a ball – I mean, it was a clear strike – and the bases were loaded and that walked in the run that won the game last night. So you see, they were cheated, and that's another reason why you should pull for the Brewers."

Go Brewers.

Suffering with the Tar Heels

Is there any suffering that can compare with that endured by the ardent fan of a winning basketball team?

I wonder.

Let me tell you about a friend of mine

He's 40, grown a bit thick in the middle, a sensitive, rational man, a devoted fan of Carolina sports, particularly basketball, a game he played quite well in his trimmer youth.

I've watched several Carolina games on TV with him this season, and despite Carolina's impressive record of 29 wins and 2 losses, I don't think I've seen him take a moment's pleasure from any game.

Such agonies I've seldom witnessed. And the despair...well, it's surely unfathomable.

His suffering begins well before the game. Take Carolina's game with Alabama in the NCAA East Regional tournament at Raleigh. He is pacing nervously before the game saying, "I don't know, Alabama, they're strong, we may just lose this one."

As player introductions begin, he turns off the sound on the TV and switches on the radio to hear Woody Durham call the game.

"Woody Durham likes Carolina," he explains.

The game has barely begun before he is wallowing in misery. "We can't do a thing," he mutters. A score by Carolina merely elicits a grunt.

"Carolina looks sluggish," he says with disgust, "real sluggish."

Carolina makes a turnover and he leaps on the back of his chair screaming words inappropriate for a family newspaper.

"Settle down," another friend says, trying to calm him.

When Alabama hits, making the score 10-6 in favor of Carolina, his despair is beyond consolation.

"Well, it's all over," he says shaking his head. "We might as well quit. Worthy can't hit. Worthy ain't doin' nothin'."

Alabama scores again. "Look at that. That's embarrassing. They're beating us at our own game.

A run of Carolina baskets draws only a sigh of relief, a grudging, "All right." But an Alabama score that brings them back within four points, gets a loud expletive and a retreat to desperation. "Well, that's just about it."

Moments later, when a freshman Carolina player loses an inbounds pass under the Alabama basket, he jumps up yelling, "Why in the hell did they give it to Martin? He can't even walk!" and stalks from the room to fix himself a drink.

By halftime, with Carolina leading by five points, he has worked himself into a delicious agony.

"I've never in my life seen anybody who gets quite as upset as you do when their team is winning," a friend observes.

"They're not playing well," he says. "Perkins ain't doin' nothin', ain't doin' a damn thing."

With the game resumed and Alabama closing the gap, his misery is beyond description. He writhes; he winces; he gasps.

"Oh man, this is awful. This is just awful. We've lost this one."

A little later, he is even yelling at Woody Durham for noting that James Worthy, about to take a foul shot, hasn't missed a free throw yet in the game.

"You psyched him out, you...," he screams at the radio when Worthy misses.

Carolina makes another turnover and he grits his teeth. "They're trying hard just to give it to 'em. I can't stand it." He stalks from the room for another drink

Two minutes, 49 seconds left in the game. Carolina has a six-point lead. Others in the room are beginning to express cautious confidence of a Carolina win.

"That's a long time, awful long time," he says. "Couple of turnovers and they're dead."

167

With less than a minute to play and Carolina maintaining its lead, others are celebrating. My friend is still tense with the dread of defeat. Not until a time out with five seconds left and Carolina leading by five does he begin to relax.

"I don't feel *absolutely* comfortable," he says, "just reasonably so."

"Well, they're going to beat Villanova, no doubt about that," somebody says after Carolina has won.

"I don't know," my friend says. "The only reason they won this one was because they were hitting the free throws. The *only* reason. They tried to give the damn thing away there at the end with those turnovers. Jimmy Black forgot he was supposed to be an extension of Dean Smith."

A Pilgrimage to the Temple

Seeing it for the first time, glowing on the hill in the light night fog, hordes of people streaming toward it, evoked visions of the spaceship in *Close Encounters of the Third Kind*, and I felt like one of those people who'd been drawn irresistibly to the alien vessel in the movie.

That was wrong, I knew. I should be feeling like a pilgrim, one among the throngs of faithful streaming to pay homage at the great temple.

A temple is what it is, the Dean Dome, the new $34-million so-called student activities center named for Dean Smith on the Chapel Hill campus of the University of North Carolina, a building big enough to comfortably seat the entire population of Asheboro, where I live, and still have room for a crowd from Randleman, Richard Petty's hometown.

There can be no question that basketball is a religious experience at Carolina and the Dean Dome is its shrine. So faithful are its followers that some, I'm told, were willing to cough up a quarter million dollars or more just for the privilege of sitting near the altar.

Although only the most privileged are allowed in the sacred sanctuary of the temple, the faithful are legion, and I had come with one of the most devoted, a man with more heart than money to contribute. Thus our admission was on windfall tickets from a friend.

This was a first visit for both of us, and we were properly awed and reverent as we climbed to our seats in the nose-bleed zone and settled down to try to adjust our ears to the pressure change.

"Should've brought my binoculars," my friend said with

a grunt, as I tried to acclimate my eyes to the blue glow. I should explain that my friend is a Carolina fan in the truest sense of the word, a fanatic. His faith, though, is not exactly that of Moses.

As soon as Maryland scored its first basket, he slumped in his seat, defeated. "Well, that's it," he said. "It's all over. We've lost this one. We might as well go home."

I'm talking the original Mr. Negative here. I've seen him uneasy with Carolina up 30 points and only two minutes left to play.

Uneasy would be a mild description of his condition as the game advanced. I kept busy trying to remember CPR techniques and to hold one hand within reach of his coattail in case, as the game grew close, he decided to end his misery with a grand leap into the high-rent district below.

"You can relax now," I said as the game entered the final three minutes with Carolina leading by nine. "Carolina's got it."

"A lot can happen in three minutes," my friend said, his face fraught with worry.

"But it hasn't happened in 37 minutes," I said, "so why should it happen in three?"

Thirty-five seconds later, a lot had happened. Carolina's lead had fallen to three and a little later it dipped to zero. Disaster came with overtime, reducing my friend to a quivering, glazed-eye heap as the result became inevitable.

"I knew it," he said. "I would have to be here for the first loss in the Dean Dome. They'll never be No. 1 again. This is the worst day of my life, the worst day of my life. I'll never get over this."

"Yes, you will," I said. "They'll turn around. Everything will be all right."

But he was inconsolable as I tried to lead him out of the temple. I was trying to lead him quickly because he had lapsed into muttered curses that were making me nervous.

"I hate Carolina," he said. "I hope they never win again. I hate Dean Smith. I hate Kenny Smith. I hate the Dean Dome. I hope the damn thing falls in."

I kept trying to shush him because we were surrounded by the faithful, and I didn't think they would take kindly to such blasphemy in the temple. I was afraid they might turn on us and stone us as heretics.

We had parked more than a mile away in a lot rife with towing warnings, and I knew that the hike back was going to be long and difficult.

"I hate fraternities," my friend muttered as I maneuvered him past a pledge selling T-shirts in the parking lot. "I hate T-shirts."

His arm made a grand sweep of the horizon. "I hate those dormitories. I hate those pine trees. I hate Chapel Hill. I don't know why I came here in the first place. I hate blue." The most positive thoughts I could conjure failed to penetrate the moroseness of his mood.

"Car's probably been towed," he said, as we neared the lot where we'd parked.

"Maybe not," I said.

"Just my luck," he said. "This is the worst day of my life, I'm telling you. The worst day of my life. We'll be here all night. I hate Dean Smith."

I was beginning to get concerned myself because the lot was in view and I couldn't spot the car.

"It's been towed, I know it," he said.

"No, it hasn't," I said excitedly. "It's there. I see it. Everything's going to be all right. I told you so."

"Bet it won't start," he said.

The Splatter Factor

Some observations left over from a visit to the Dean Dome, UNC's new basketball temple at Chapel Hill.

It really is an impressive structure, seemingly built in a pit dug into the top of a hill. It will seat a lot of people, more than 21,000. And while all the seats offer reasonably good vantage points, you couldn't call the seating exactly comfortable.

If a basketball player, or any other excessively tall person, tried to watch a game from one of the seats, the person in front of him would need a fondness for ear muffs, because that's the purpose his knees would serve. And a person of any great width might find it difficult to get into one of the seats at all.

Other than that, the only real problem is the same one found in all monstrous buildings: the toilets. The big problem here, of course, is that everybody wants to go at the same time – halftime. No architect has ever been able to deal effectively with that problem.

Yet it's clear that some thought was given to it in the design of the Dean Dome, at least in the men's room, which is different from any that I've been in before.

In appearance, the men's room is an awful vision of the future, appropriate to the spaceship look of the building. One long wall is taken up with what appears to be a stainless steel waterfall with a narrow catch basin at the bottom. This clearly was designed to accommodate the most people possible in the briefest amount of time, and for that it functions well.

Only one flaw mars the design. Call it the splatter factor.

The automatic flow of water over the fall is such that if you get close enough to the apparatus to take care of business, you're certain to get splattered. If you stay far enough back to keep from getting wet, you could find yourself unable to take care of business in an acceptable manner. The sinks, too, are of unusual design. They protrude from the walls, huge, round and flat, looking as if they were cut from stone. In the center of each is a small round pedestal. Push a button on the wall and tiny watergun-like streams of water spray out of the pedestal in every direction.

These little sprays of water are inadequate to any serious hand washing. And when a crowd is gathered around the sink (I don't guess you could accurately call it a sink anymore, it being flat, with only a little railing to contain the water), all the little steams are simply deflected onto those nearby. Coming away from the thing without being splashed is dang nigh impossible.

While you have to give somebody credit for effort in men's room design, these are problems sufficient to take back to the drawing board.

I can't speak, of course, to any problems in the women's room, never having ventured there. It's clear from the long lines outside that facility at halftime that there definitely is a problem that hasn't been dealt with adequately.

Considering the basic differences in men and women and the extra premium that women place on privacy, it may be that it is impossible to deal with the problem of moving large numbers of people in and out quickly without drastically increasing the space allotted.

This not only gets into economics, but could bring up matters of sexual discrimination, subjects I'd just as not get into. These, after all, are just a few observations about a fine new building that should make every Carolina fan proud.

And speaking of Carolina fans, let me offer one more little story about my friend Mr. Negative, the ultimate Carolina fan of little faith.

During a close Carolina-Georgia Tech game in Atlanta my friend, watching at home on TV, suffered such agonies of negativism that even Carolina's 1-point victory could not alleviate them.

The next day, he happened to be at lunch with a group of

friends in an establishment that had the TV tuned to ESPN's replay of the game. As the game came down to the crunch, my friend couldn't help himself

"They're going to lose," he started moaning. "I know it."

Go Super Bowl(ing)

Just when you begin to think that newspapers have covered every angle of the Super Bowl that the human imagination can conceive, danged if they don't manage to come up with something else.

On the Friday before the game, for example, one of North Carolina's major newspapers presented its readers with a long story offering suggestions for things to do for people who, for whatever perverted and un-American reasons, choose not to watch the game on TV. The very first suggestion: Go bowling.

Wouldn't you like to know the thought process behind that article?

Did the editors think that anybody who isn't caught up in the excitement of the Super Bowl is so pathetically out of touch, so hopelessly incompetent as to be unable to think of a single thing to do for two hours while the rest of the nation sits enthralled before TV watching overfed guys without necks piling atop one another?

"Well, Mable, if we don't watch this here ball game, what will we do? We can't just set here, can we?"

"Get the paper, peahead, and see if it won't tell us something."

"Says here to go bowling."

"Well, I reckon we better."

Of course, some may argue and the evidence seems strong, that the media get so caught up in Super Bowl hoopla that they will grasp at anything, no matter how stupid, to keep it going – even to the point of attempting to send innocent people bowling.

Bowling I will not be come kickoff. I expect to be doing

the same thing I have done during previous Super Bowls. Which is almost anything other than watching it – with the exception, that is, of bowling.

I don't know that I can offer an acceptable reason for having never seen a Super Bowl game other than that watching football seems only little more exciting to me than watching golf, and not nearly as interesting as a TV fishing show. Another reason is that I can't find any reason to pull for a professional football team, and few sports are interesting if you aren't pulling for somebody.

I know that a lot of people hereabouts pull for the Washington Redskins, who happen to be playing in today's game. Once, in my far distant youth, I had some of those sympathies myself. That was because Choo-Choo Justice played for the Redskins, and he was from North Carolina.

Come to think of it, I don't think I've watched a professional football game since Choo-Choo retired.

If something drastic happened that forced me to watch today's game (say somebody offered me a large sum of money, or held a gun to my head), I might pull for the Redskins just for sentimental reasons.

But that would be morally wrong. At least, that's what a friend tells me.

"The Redskins are obnoxious scumbags," she said. "I hate the Redskins They are puke."

If I am to pull for anybody, said my friend – who as you may have guessed is from Colorado – it should be for the Broncos, because they are "nice guys."

I don't know much about football, but I do know it ain't exactly a parlor game, and if I were putting money on a game and had to choose between a bunch of nice guys and a gang of obnoxious scumbags, I'd go with the scumbags even though I wanted the nice guys to win.

The Denver fans are another reason I should pull for the Broncos, my friend told me. They are so dedicated to their team and its colors – orange and blue – that they go to unusual lengths to encourage them.

One fan painted her horse orange and her body blue and

rode naked down a Denver Street the other day, my friend said. Another ate a bowlful of live goldfish and a tubful of squirming blue worms.

Now if I could be assured that the Denver fans would be doing that kind of stuff along the sidelines during the game, I might be inclined to watch it.

Short of that, though, the only thing that might cause me to watch would be an announcement that Dan Rather was suiting up for the Broncos and George Bush would be playing with the Redskins.

Actually, I just want the game to be over so there will be something else to read about in the newspapers. At one point last week, you couldn't turn to any section of the paper without finding Super Bowl stories. Even the food section was offering players' favorite dishes.

Incidentally, in case you missed it and would like to try it, here is Redskins linebacker Dave Butz's recipe for steak:

Tackle a cow. Tear off its leg. Eat.

The Benefits of Not Coaching

One of my big problems in life, I can see now – too late, alas, at this advanced stage – is that I never had proper vocational counseling.

Come to think of it, I don't recall ever having any vocational counseling at all, which may explain why I am in my present line of work. But even if I had had vocational counseling I'd probably still be upset about it, knowing what I know now, because apparently there is a lot of really attractive work out there that counselors aren't telling people about.

I'm talking about work for which even I would be qualified that not only is much easier than what I'm doing but pays a heck of a lot more.

For example, if I had it to do all over, instead of going into the column writing business, I think I'd take up not coaching football.

Now there is an easy job if I ever heard of one. It sounds almost as easy as being one of those farmers that the government pays not to grow cotton or peanuts.

Just the kind of job I've dreamed about. And when it comes to not coaching football, I think I'd be as qualified as the next guy.

In fact, I'm sure that I'm more qualified than many because I don't care one whit about football. I never pay attention to it. Don't think about it at all. Surely never thinking about football would be a big advantage to not coaching it.

The big reason I would want to not coach football is not because it's so easy, though, but because it pays so well.

I was flabbergasted to discover just how much it does pay. I had no idea that it could be so lucrative.

But one day I read in the newspaper where somebody named Dick Crum, I believe it was, is being paid $800,000 not to coach football at the University of North Carolina at Chapel Hill for the next four years.

As soon as I read that, I got out a pen and did a little figuring. That was when I began to see the error in my choice of careers.

Not coaching football for just four years pays considerably more, I can tell you, than writing newspaper columns week in and week out for more than 20 years.

Is it any wonder I'm so upset?

Why, not coaching football for four years pays as much as teaching high school for 35 or 40 years – a whole career – and that includes grading an awful lot of papers.

As amazing as it may sound to people who actually have to do something for their paychecks, not coaching football pays more than coaching it. According to the news, this guy Crum was being paid only $87,000 a year for coaching, but he is getting $200,000 a year for not doing it.

To those of us who have no concern at all for football, except when it is pre-empting a favorite TV show, that makes contorted sense, because anybody who is doing something to keep football from being seen deserves more than somebody who is helping to perpetrate it.

But even to us contorted thinkers, being paid more for not doing something than for doing it still seems a touch topsy-turvy somehow.

The problem with getting one of these high-paying jobs not coaching football, I quickly discovered, is that you actually have to coach it first.

There's always a catch to every sweet-sounding deal, I guess. Otherwise, everybody would be getting rich not coaching something.

Once you have managed to get a fairly well-paying job coaching football, the secret to getting one of those much higher paying jobs not coaching is to not coach very well.

Does that make sense? Doesn't sound as if it should, I know, but that's precisely the case.

Coaches who do poor jobs and lose games are rewarded with the far easier duties and much bigger bucks available in not coaching.

With a system like that, you'd think that a smart coach would pull every trick he could think of to lose. Yet for some reason you still see coaches striving all the time to win.

Makes you wonder, doesn't it?

Think it could have something to with all that head-knocking in football?

Only in the South

Storming the Supermarkets

People who move to these parts from colder climes are often astonished upon first witnessing the phenomenon that occurs when a snowfall of any consequence is expected.

Let one of the TV weather guys mention the possibility of more than an inch of snow and the immediate reaction of the natives is always the same: "Quick, let's rush out and empty the supermarkets!"

And that, of course, is precisely what we do.

Ever seen or heard any news reports about local snowstorms that didn't mention "panic buying" of groceries?

I can only imagine what it must be like for the poor people who work at supermarkets. They must feel a little like the defenders of the Alamo did when they looked out and saw all those Mexicans.

We all descend upon the supermarkets at once and charge pell-mell into the fray, scrambling to grab whatever we can. The far-outnumbered clerks, cashiers and baggers are utterly defenseless.

By the time the the news crews arrive, the employees are blank-eyed with exhaustion and showing all the symptoms of shell shock. The cameras always sweep along the bread shelves and milk coolers, and they always are empty. Not one crust of bread. Not one tiny carton of milk.

No matter how much bread and milk the bakeries and dairies produce, it never can be enough to see Carolinians through a snowstorm. If we are going to have to endure snow, we can do it only with the comfort of excesses of milk and bread.

And it's not just milk and bread we must have. We want

all kinds of food, and we want lots of it. If we have to look out the window and see snow or ice, we want to be able to look in the fridge and the kitchen cabinets and see food enough to last at least until the Fourth of July. Surely, we figure, the thaw will have set in by then.

I plead as guilty as the rest.

When I left work early one Friday because snow was predicted instinct took me straight to the supermarket. I always have stockpiled food to some extent, and with the food we had on hand, if Linda and I were somehow trapped at home with no access to the outside world, not even from an emergency air drop, we probably wouldn't be threatened with genuine hunger at least until summer.

We were running low on a few items, but I couldn't say we really needed anything. Snow was coming, though, and I felt obligated by my heritage to join in a supermarket raid.

I would just pick up a few things, I told myself, but when I arrived at the store where I often shop, I hardly could find a parking spot. People actually were running toward the place, as if they were afraid that unless they hurried nothing would be left.

I got inside only to discover a group of people standing near the entrances looking bewildered, because not a single cart was available. Every checkout counter was in service, and the lines reached all the way to the back of the store. There was hardly room to push a cart if you could have gotten one. A few people actually were pushing one cart while pulling another – and both were piled so high with food that you'd have thought these people were laying in stores for a Klondike winter.

Spring was only a month away. Surely we wouldn't be frozen in until then, but with the food they had in their carts some of these people could have fed the Green Bay Packers for a month. In all my years in North Carolina, I've never been trapped at home by weather for more than five days, and this storm, too, surely would pass within a couple of days and the supermarkets would still be there, their supplies replenished.

I stood at the door for a few minutes, awestruck by the sight. Did I really want to submit myself to this mob scene just for a head of cabbage, a box of tea, a few cans of dog food? I knew I wouldn't be able to get bread and milk to bring me any real comfort, because it surely was gone already. And even if I were able to get it, by the time I got through one of these lines, would the snow be too deep for me to get it home?

No, I didn't want to submit myself to such an ordeal. I turned around and left, and on the way I tried to figure out what it is that causes us to respond this way to just a little snow.

Does something in our blood hark back to hard times at the end of the Civil War – when our ancestors scratched through the winters eating roots and wild greens and whatever game they could kill – and cause us to hoard for harsh times?

Whatever the reasons for this insecurity, I needn't have indulged it. We ate very well during the two days we were snowed in. And when I went back to the supermarket Monday, it still was there – and even had plenty of milk and bread.

Newcomers from the north laugh at us for the way we react to snow, you know. They find it so amusing they even call back home and tell their friends about it.

They are right, of course, hard as it is to admit. When it comes to snow, we Southerners go slap crazy.

The Flop-Out Mule

Recent efforts by myself and fellow columnist Jim Jenkins, chronicling activities of certain members of the rodent family, inspired Alvin Scott of Siler City to take to his typewriter and pound out a critter story of his own.

OK, so it isn't about a mouse or a rat or even a 'possum or armadillo, but if a couple of rodent stories can serve as inspiration for a good mule-tale, that's all to the good.

Unfortunately, Alvin was so inspired and is such a stylish storyteller that he wrote at a length too great to allow me to offer the full account here in his own words. I have, regrettably, had to condense.

The story begins in the spring of 1948 when Alvin was about to turn 17 and living with his family on a farm near Ridgeway, Va., just above the North Carolina line on U.S. 220. Alvin's father decided they needed a good mule to help work the place and entrusted Alvin with the job of driving a borrowed truck to the monthly mule sale in Asheboro and bringing back a big, healthy, gentle and hard-working mule.

Disappointed to discover only small, pony-like mules at the sale, Alvin expressed his dismay at finding none of the sort his father wanted to a silver-haired gentleman in bib overalls who looked to be "the epitome of honesty and integrity."

"My new found friend explained very carefully and in a gentle voice that he had such a mule at home," Alvin wrote, "and the reason that he hadn't brought the animal to the sale today was that he didn't want it to catch any germs or diseases from all these ol' trader mules that had been brung to the sale."

Alvin went to look at the mule and was very impressed, but he had only $100 to spend. After due consideration, the old fellow said he guessed he could take a loss. They loaded up the mule and Alvin drove it home.

Let Alvin pick up the story here: "Early next morning, after the mule had eaten 10 ears of yellow corn and drunk a No. 2 wash tub of hand-wound well water, and I had eaten two large buttermilk biscuits, along with three Rhode Island Red hen eggs over easy and three strips of crispy fried fat back meat, along with several spoonsful of sopping milk gravy – and a cup of H&C Coffee, we were ready for some heavy duty garden ploughing.

At this point, Alvin wanders off the subject a bit to talk about H&C Coffee and the glories of spring but finally gets back to the mule.

"Here we were, a young family with a new farm, a new mule, a large mortgage and spring of the year! Let's plow, and plow we did! We plowed till we had a strip across the garden about 10 feet wide. Then our new mule laid down! Right in the garden!

"At first, we thought we had fed him too much – surely we hadn't worked him too hard. Try as I might, this mule just wasn't going to get up. It wasn't until later that I learned I had been sold what is known in the trade as a North Carolina flop-out mule.

"No doubt, you have seen people like this. After they work just a little bit, they just lay down and flop out. That's the way it was with this mule. I went to the house and got two oatmeal cookies and a glass of cold sweet milk. While I was having my snack, the mule, lying out there in the garden in the warm spring sun, went to sleep.

"Now, high up in the sky a big ol' buzzard was flying around, looking for what buzzard's look for. The buzzard saw what appeared to be a dead mule flopped out in the garden. With a big swoop, the buzzard lit at the edge of the garden and from my vantage point at the kitchen window, I saw the buzzard cautiously walk around the sound asleep mule.

"This buzzard, a bird of affluent and refined dining, walked around to the rear of the mule and took a big bite out of what would be the center-cut ham section of a hog.

"Hee haw! The mule came alive! Frightened, mortified and stupefied, the poor mule leaped to his feet, his tail high in the air. The buzzard had his teeth buried into the tender flesh. The mule's tail came down and caught the buzzard's neck, and the choking buzzard was flapping his wings vainly trying to get away.

"Of course, this frightened the mule all the more and he ran away. Around and around our farm, the mule and buzzard went, dragging the mole board plow behind, ripping, tearing, plowing and harrowing the entire 65-acre farm in just 14 minutes flat.

"The mule finally stubbed his toe on a rock, and as he fell, his tail came up, the buzzard got loose and flew away. We finally got the mule calmed down.

"We kept that ol' mule three more years and sold him to a neighbor and they kept him 10 years, and that ol' mule never laid down again as long as he lived. The day the mule died, he went out in the woods, leaned up against a pine tree and expired."

The Yankee Chickens Are Coming!

The Great American Chicken War is what it's being called in some quarters, including, I suppose, even breast quarters and thigh quarters. It erupted over this question: Should chicken be yellow?

But in North Carolina, the fight is taking on more emotional colorings: blue and gray.

Or to put it in a more alarming way: The Yankee chickens are coming! The Yankee chickens are coming!

Actually, the Yankee chickens are already here, and they are seizing more and more territory, namely in supermarket meat cases. That obviously has alarmed the folks who produce our proud Southern chickens, which are not, by Beauregard, yellow.

"Yellow Bellied Chicken?" the full-page ad asks disdainfully.

That is how this war is being fought, incidentally—in TV and newspaper ads.

The combatants are Holly Farms, which has firm North Carolina roots and claims to produce "the official chicken of the South (and anywhere else that counts)," and Perdue Farms, the invader from you-know-where, which, curiously, claims to produce spoiled chickens.

Perdue Farms, with headquarters in Maryland, is run by one Frank Perdue, who, like certain car dealers and carpet salesmen, likes to appear in his own TV commercials. He has become very famous in these parts lately with an advertising blitz for his yellow chickens.

Every time I see this guy on TV going on about what fine houses his chickens live in, I expect him to begin scratching the ground and clucking and maybe even fly onto the roof of the chicken house to cock-a-doodle-doo. If any salesman ever began to look like his product, it surely has to be this guy Perdue.

Perdue even runs his picture with his newspaper ads, and across it is this line – "It takes a tough man to make a tender chicken." But that line across that picture is somehow less than convincing, and so, frankly, are the wordy Perdue ads.

From the ads, you'd think that Perdue was in the chicken resort business rather than the business of raising and slaughtering hapless chickens for the dinner table.

"The way to make great chickens is to spoil them," Perdue crows.

Then he goes on at great length about how his chickens "live a life of luxury" and "eat prince's meals." When Perdue talks about the $90,000 houses (without land) that his chickens live in, you get the idea that they must be carpeted in plush pile and outfitted with grand chandeliers and Jacuzzis. Each has a 500-foot picture window so the chickens can enjoy the view and plenty of living space so that each chicken can "make friends, or find a quiet place of its own."

"A tense chicken is likely to end up being tough," says Perdue, so he does everything he can to keep his chickens calm, including soothing them with music when they get excited and seeing that they get plenty of sleep.

"Perdue chickens eat better than you do," he says (even if you eat only Perdue chicken?).

Their diet is "like a menu from a health-food store." It includes fish "straight from the Chesapeake Bay," plus specially ground soybean meal and yellow corn, corn gluten and marigold petals. The latter three give the chicken its "golden-yellow color."

The marigolds, incidentally, are "still hand-picked – petal by petal!" Petal by petal? Must take an awful long time to pick those boogers. You'd think it hardly worth all that effort just to turn chickens yellow.

The purpose of all of this pampering, according to Perdue, is to make a tender chicken. But if a tense chicken is a tough chicken, it seems to me that all of this pampering must be wasted, because no matter how luxuriously these chickens live, in the end, somebody's going to come in one night, snatch them up by their feet, jam them into crowded coops and haul them off to chop off their heads and make sure they are yellow inside. If I were a chicken, I think I'd be tense under those conditions.

Holly Farms, in its counter assault against the Perdue invasion, doesn't mess with wordy treatises on chicken pampering or any other folderol. It goes straight for the gut, relying on old fears and prejudices.

"Heard there's a chicken farmer up North who swears chicken should be yellow," its full-page ad says. "That's right. Yellow. Like a banana. Worse still, he's trying out those yellow chickens down here.

"Now maybe up there they color-code their food so they can find it easier. They do things differently up there. Which is fine. For them. But down here..."

Notice all this business about "up there" and "down here." The message is clear. Yankees are crazy enough to eat anything. But we smart, loyal Southerners just ain't gonna hold with yeller chicken.

I say score one for the chickens in gray.

Looking Down on Neighbors

I saw where a writer for the *Los Angeles Times* has discovered that not only are all Southerners not alike, as your basic non-Southerner is apt to think, but lots of Southerners don't even like one another.

"Scratch a Southerner," writes David Treadwell, "and you'll find a dedicated states rightist – dedicated to the right to look down on his neighbor states. Wherever, you go in Dixie, from the redneck bars of Georgia to the blue-blood parlors of Virginia, state chauvinism is an enduring feature of the Southern way of life."

As an example, he cites a resident of Atlanta who dislikes Alabamians so much that he wants to stomp the speakers when a certain tune about Alabama comes on the juke box.

It isn't surprising that in a mean-spirited state filled with chicken pluckers and watermelon seed suckers, where the top IQs rarely equal the temperature on an average summer day, where every other person is named Bo and even the BMWs in Atlanta have gun racks in the rear windows, that it wouldn't be hard to find people who look down on their neighbors for no better reason than that they eat their peanuts with the hulls still on, give towns names like Opp and erect monuments to boll weevils, all of which Alabamians are guilty.

But isn't that a little like a skunk not wanting to live next to a paper mill because it stinks?

I mean, that is just the kind of thing you'd expect from people in Alabama and Georgia, but is it any reason to jump to the conclusion that people in all states of the South think and act in the same way?

Hardly.

Certainly, it isn't true of North Carolinians, even though we realize, of course, that all of our neighbors are less than perfect.

We are keenly aware, for example, that Virginians are afflicted with an undeserved and unbearable haughtiness that causes so many of them to hold their noses so high in the air that a good rain shower could drown much of the population, as I think I may have previously noted. But we know that the delusion of Virginians is based in visions of an illustrious past that has nothing to do with present reality – which is that all the best Virginians long ago saw the light and migrated to North Carolina.

But does that cause us to look down on our northern neighbors? Not in the least. We feel sorry for Virginians. We would do anything we could to help relieve them of their pathetic hallucinations of a grandeur none of them ever knew. But we couldn't bring ourselves to look down on them for it any more than we could blame a mule for being stubborn. It's something they can't help. It's in the blood.

It's the same with our unfortunate neighbors in that scrubland to the south that shares our state's name. We could point out that it is mainly a haven for palmettos, pellagra and possum chasers, where a chitlin strut is considered an elegant social event, where the idea of the ultimate artistic expression takes the form of a humongous monument to the peach that more closely resembles an elephant's behind, where ultimate intellectual comment is thought to be a shout of "Go Tigers!" We could do that, but we are too well mannered for it even to cross our minds.

In his article, Treadwell inadvertently touches on the reason that we can't bring ourselves to look down on our neighbors. He quotes that old line dating back to colonial times about North Carolina being "a vale of humility between two mountains of conceit."

I never quite agreed with that description. North Carolinians were never humble. They were just so cantankerous and independent and content with what they'd found that they didn't bother to acknowledge the conceited blue noses in

Charleston and Richmond who considered them less than civilized.

Nevertheless, Treadwell continues to perpetuate the fallacy that North Carolina "long found it hard to hold its head high" admidst the arrogance of its neighbors. But now, he notes, "once lowly North Carolina has emerged from its relative obscurity to surpass both Virginia and South Carolina" and he goes on to cite statistics to prove it.

Well, North Carolinians never had any trouble holding their heads high and certainly never thought of their state as lowly for the simple reason that they knew from the beginning that they had found the fairest place this side of heaven and that our neighbors could never hope to have anything to compare. That we are now proving ourselves to be statistically superior is utterly irrelevant for we have known all along where we stood. And confidence in that knowledge is the reason we could never bring ourselves to look down on anybody.

Only those who secretly believe themselves inferior resort to such distasteful behavior.

From Giant Collards
to Frustrated Flamingos

Walking in Tall Collards

Am I the only one who's noticed that the world seems to tilt slightly out of kilter during the holidays? I mean, screwy things go on. Just about every day I've notice new developments in the newspaper.

A couple of days before Christmas I saw this headline: "Collards Become Giant With Help of Chickens."

Who could resist a story like that? How does a collard become a giant? What did the chickens do to help? Just how big is a giant collard anyway?

Well, first of all, the chickens probably didn't realize they were helping. Their contribution was of an involuntary nature.

How big is a giant collard? Ten feet tall.

Friends, that is a big collard. I have grown collards three feet tall, maybe even close to four feet, but 10 feet is colossal in collards. We are talking shade collards here. Timber collards.

These collards were grown by neighbors in Pensacola, Fla. Rose Gainer said she got her seeds from California, which might explain their perversion, but Moton and Myrtle Hurry said theirs were just "plain ol' Georgia collards."

All three had grown collards before but none like these. The only thing they did differently this time was to use chicken manure as fertilizer.

Just below that story was another headline that said, "Crop of Super Trees on the Way." This story told of researchers injecting trees with a special hormone that causes them to grow at incredible rates.

Think about what might happen if they also used chicken manure as fertilizer for these trees. Then consider what the effect could be if they injected giant collards with this hormone.

You could feed whole cities with a single collard. Come to think about it, considering the general appeal of collards, I guess there are cities now you could feed with a single collard – a regular one.

Anyway, this whole giant collard business is something for the town of Ayden in eastern North Carolina to look into. That's the town that holds the collard festival every year. Imagine a town with every street veiled by stately collards. And if anybody there got hungry all he'd have to do is saw off a limb and boil it a week or two.

The subject of growing things brings up another unusual story that appeared during the holidays. Duke University apparently is aswarm with bald-headed folks who are taking part in a hair-growing experiment. Researchers have been rubbing their heads with a high blood pressure medicine called minoxidil. It's causing many of them to grow hair, although not always a full healthy crop. I wonder if they've considered mixing that stuff with chicken manure?

But let's not get away from trees just yet. Another recent story out of Oregon told about teams of U.S. government-employed tree counters. That's right, tree counters. They go around counting trees for the Forest Service.

The trouble was that they didn't tell exactly how they do it. I have trouble counting half a dozen oranges in a plastic sack at the supermarket. How could you possibly go into a forest and start counting without getting confused? After 15 minutes, how would you know which ones you'd counted and which ones you hadn't? Trees look pretty much alike, don't they?

Oh, well. Screwy things are going on, I'm telling you. Look at some other things that have happened in the past few days.

An exterminator in Chicago killed himself by drinking rat poison.

In California, two sea lions named Joyce and Faye are being trained as life guards.

In Jefferson City, Mo., the assistant majority leader of the

House in the Missouri Legislature has proposed making nose blowing illegal in restaurants in the state. He thinks that nose blowing is "gross" and potentially unhealthy and that may be true. But is it as gross and unhealthy as the alternative: not blowing and dribbling?

The Communist Party in China proposed doing away with chopsticks in favor of forks. This is an outrage that only a bunch of communists or fundamentalists preachers would try to pull. No doubt, the commies suspect that the Chinese people are enjoying their food too much.

Everybody who knows anything about Chinese food knows that it tastes better with chopsticks. Must be something about the way Chinese food interacts with metal. I know that some people will say this is silly, but these will be the same people who will tell you that a big Coke tastes the same as the little one. It just ain't so.

A fellow in Ft. Lauderdale, Fla., who guaranteed to take messages to the hereafter for $20 died after memorizing messages from more than 30 people who paid for the service. The shortest message was from a fellow who'd been left out of his father's will: "Why Dad?" What I want to know is who's going to bring back the answer?

Counting Sheep

I'm not sure why it is, but for some reason I'm attracted to odd little stories in the news. Like that one hidden on an inside page of the newspaper about a woman dying in Jordan who was reported to be 165 years old.

Living to such an advanced age is a notable enough achievement, but this woman, whose name was Noffa Saas Khalaf, accomplished something that was even more remarkable, it seems to me.

A newspaper in Amman, where this woman died last Wednesday, was quoted as saying that she "lived a normal life, smoked cigarettes, had a strong body and excellent memory and ate half a sheep a day."

Ate half a sheep a day? This is a normal life? I know people who have led what I would consider to be relatively normal lives without ever eating even a lamb chop.

Think of it. That's 182 sheep a year. If this woman maintained such eating habits since young adulthood, say her midteens, she would have put away more than 27,000 sheep in her lifetime.

That's a sizable flock, no matter how you look at it. I can remember lying awake most of a night counting sheep without chalking up much more than a thousand. Imagine eating 27,000 of the critters. You'd think it would take a normal person more than 165 years of steady eating to work through that many sheep without taking any smoking breaks at all.

I checked an encyclopedia and learned that an average sheep may weigh anywhere from 100 to 200 pounds. Say 150. I don't know what that would dress out to. A hundred pounds maybe? Let's say that.

That leaves 50 pounds to the side. Cooking would bring some shrinkage. What, 20 percent? OK, discount bones and gristle for another 50 percent. That still leaves a good 20 pounds of cooked mutton a day.

I may not be normal, but I have trouble getting through a half-pound ribeye at dinner. If I had to face 20 pounds of cooked mutton every day, I'm almost certain that I wouldn't want to live to be 65, much less 165.

Even if this woman slept only four hours a day, she'd still have to choke down a pound an hour. Surely nobody, no matter how great a mutton glutton, could eat only mutton hour after hour.

Didn't she ever throw in any bread or vegetables or banana pudding to break the monotony? You know she must have. That would have stretched out her eating time even more, not to mention her belly.

Did she get any sleep at all? And just how big was that strong body of hers anyway? It must've been enormous. She might have been the world's largest person as well as the oldest. And don't you suppose she had to hold the world's record for sheep eating?

Not a word of any of that was in the news story, though. That's the trouble with these little hidden-away stories. They never tell you enough.

How did this woman get all those sheep in the first place? She couldn't have had time to raise them, what with all that time she had to spend eating. Or to cook them either, for that matter.

It must take six or eight hours to cook half a sheep. Who cooked them for her, and how did she prefer them? Stewed? Barbecued?

Did her teeth hold up, or was somebody having to put all that mutton through a blender and make mush out of it in her later years?

What about that clear memory of hers? What could she possibly remember other than sheep?

Was there any one sheep that stood out in her mind, maybe a particularly tender ewe back in 1842, when she was a young woman of 24?

And how did she find time to smoke cigarettes? Could she smoke and eat at the same time?

Some reporters just never think to ask the right questions, I guess.

The Critter Who Came to Dinner

My friend Ellie Craig was having a big dinner party at her house, so two friends, Ellen Emerson and Ann Clegg, went over to help her get ready for it.

They were setting the house in order when Ellen and Ann took a load of stuff up to the attic to stash it temporarily.

Suddenly, Ellie heard a commotion and went to investigate. Ann came fleeing down the stairs. Ellen hovered near the top of the steps.

"Ellie!" she called down excitedly. "You've got a 'possum up here."

"Oh, my heavens," said Ellie.

"We had heard some scratching up there," Ellie explained later. "I thought it was a squirrel that had got in up there and then found its way out."

Ellie has a bad hip, but she climbed up to investigate.

The critter was beside a box of old toys.

"It was just lying on its side, and its little tail was sticking out," she recalled later. She knew immediately that the tail didn't belong to a 'possum.

"That's not a 'possum," she said. "That's a raccoon."

"Possum, raccoon, it's all the same," said Ellen.

A raccoon made sense to Ellie. One night she had looked out on her front porch and seen three baby raccoons – right on Sylvan Road in the center of Greensboro. But she still couldn't imagine what a raccoon would be doing in her attic.

Ellie didn't want to risk getting too close to this one. If it was just dozing, she was afraid she would startle it, and in its fright it might lunge for her. With her bad hip, she wouldn't be able to move fast enough to get away.

She found some old cake plates from the days when she ran a cake-decorating business, and keeping her distance, she started tossing them in the direction of the critter. She wasn't trying to hit it, mind you, just hoping to make the plates land close enough to wake it and perhaps encourage it to seek other accommodations.

The critter didn't budge.

"I think it's dead," Ellie said.

She started looking around for a curtain rod – a long one – so that she could punch it and see if it was indeed dead, but she was having trouble finding one.

"Ellie, its eye blinked," Ellen cried, interrupting the search. "It's not dead."

That settled it. No need to keep looking for a curtain rod. She wasn't about to provoke a raccoon in a closed area. No telling what might happen if it thought itself trapped and decided to fight its way out.

"What on earth am I going to do?" Ellie said. "I've got all these people coming tonight. I can't have that thing up here."

She could just picture all of her guests seated for dinner, the main course just served, and a raccoon comes strolling into the dining room. Why, it might set off a panic and end up like one of those scenes in a wild comedy movie.

She and Ellen retreated down the stairs where Ann waited anxiously. They made sure to close the door so that the raccoon couldn't follow. Then they debated what to do. Call the fire department? The rescue squad? The animal control officer?

"I'll just call Ryan," Ellie said.

Ryan is her son. He was at work at Carolina Camera Center.

"But Mom..." he kept saying as she went over the situation.

"Ryan, you've got to come and get this thing out of here," she insisted, and he finally relented.

Ann volunteered to go get him, while Ellie and Ellen stood guard, giggling over how three grown women could be cowed by such a little animal.

Ryan arrived and tramped upstairs shaking his head. He was back quickly, carrying the critter. Without warning, he flung it toward his mother. She screamed and leaped back – as a raccoon hand puppet sprawled at her feet.

"I was thinking about tying it to my leg and running screaming down the stairs," Ryan said when they all had recovered from the shock and laughter.

The raccoon ended up a guest at the dinner party after all, perched atop the woodpile next to the fireplace. Ellie still laughs every time she thinks about it.

"I never felt so stupid in my life," she says. Made a great dinner party story, though.

Flamingo Love

I bumped into a friend the other day whom I hadn't seen for a while, and after we'd exchanged greetings he said, "What have you been up to?"

"Still about six-three," I said, as he winced.

"I meant activity-wise."

"Oh. Well, I've been thinking a lot about flamingos lately."

"Surely, you're not thinking about buying some of those tacky pink flamingos for your yard," he said.

"Tacky?" I said. "Tacky? How can you call a thing of sheer beauty tacky? No, I've not been thinking of buying a pair of yard flamingos. I already have a very nice set, thank you. And, moreover, I think you'll find that pink flamingos is redundant. All flamingos are pink, except those that are red, which, I submit, is simply a strong pink."

"I beg your pardon," he said.

"It's all right," I said.

"If I may be so presumptuous as to ask," he went on, "what is it that you have been thinking about flamingos?"

"Actually, I've not been thinking so much about flamingos in general as flamingos in specific. Specifically the 70 flamingos at Parrot Jungle near Miami. Did you know they went 48 years without attempting to breed?"

"I suppose you're going to tell me Jim Jenkins is trying to break their record."

"Oh, no. The man is striving daily to find the mother of his children. But the way things are going, I don't know. The flamingos still have a few years on him. "

"Forty-eight years is an awfully long time," my friend

said. "You could build up a lot of tension in that time."

"Indeed. The thing was that nobody could figure out why the birds wouldn't mate."

"Well, when you think about it, you know, don't you wonder how they ever do it in the first place? I mean, they're always standing around on one leg. I think if I tried to get amorous on one leg, I'd just fall over. It would take a delicate sense of balance, don't you think?"

Not only that," I said, "but consider those necks. They curve all around and go on forever. Flamingos have the longest necks and legs in proportion to body size of any birds on earth, you know. By the time you got through with the neck kissing, you'd be too worn out for anything else."

"You've got a point there," my friend said.

"But listen to this," I said. "A flamingo's beak is designed to work upside down. A flamingo feeds by filtering algae and other organisms out of water with its tongue. A flamingo has a remarkable tongue. It works like a piston, sucking in water and spewing it out at an amazing rate."

"I think I'm getting turned on," my friend said.

"Imagine French kissing upside down. Wouldn't be easy."

"Makes you wonder how there are any flamingos at all, doesn't it?"

"In the wild, they manage OK. In Africa some colonies number nearly a million pairs. It's just that the 35 pairs at Parrot Jungle never seemed to take an interest in each other. Nobody ever was able to figure out why until a couple of years ago. That was when Jerome Scherr, the president of Parrot Jungle, stopped having parades at the park. The flamingos soon started showing an interest in each other."

"Parades never did much for me either," said my friend. "I never had any luck with a woman I took to a parade."

"Next, this guy Scherr found out that rainstorms sometimes triggered mating in flamingos, and he turned his lawn sprinklers on them. That was all it took. Twenty-two pairs produced eggs last year, and according to a story I just read in the paper, the flamingos at Parrot Jungle are mating like crazy this spring. Complete with zany rituals such as extending their necks and shaking violently, is the way the story put it, I believe."

"I guess you would shake a little after 48 years," my friend said.

"Lot of frustration built up, I guess," I said.

"By the way," said my friend, "has anybody told Jenkins about this?"

"I called to let him know, but somebody said he'd gone out to buy a lawn sprinkler."

A Hard Act to Swallow

All towns and cities like to have some distinguishing fact about which they can boast, and a few North Carolina municipalities have been coming up with some unusual ones of late.

A couple of months back, for example, came the announcement that people in Charlotte suck up more ketchup per capita than people in any other city in the world. This came right on the heels of a report that folks in Wilmington eat more fast food per capita than people in any other city except for Odessa, Texas, and no doubt the hamburger-taco-and-fried-chicken scarfers of Wilmington are now stuffing themselves with renewed vigor in an effort to become No. 1. (Burlington, incidentally, ranks eighth in this particular competition.)

Now Durham has reached its own peculiar state of distinction. A new medical report has determined that Durham is the world's toothbrush-swallowing capital. Thirteen percent of all the incidents of toothbrush swallowing recorded throughout history occurred in Durham within the past three years.

The researchers discovered that the first recorded toothbrush swallowing happened in Hong Kong in 1882, but no details were provided. A Russian mental patient is the all-time individual champion in this activity. He ate 16 toothbrushes in 1984 without even making the *Guinness Book of World Records*.

Of the 31 incidents of toothbrush swallowing discovered by researchers, however, four were in Durham. The researchers didn't speculate about the cause of this, although they did note that "This problem should probably not be considered endemic to this part of North Carolina."

Still there has to be a reason. Could it be something in the water? Is Durham's water so slick that it causes toothbrushes to skid off teeth and tongue and careen out of control right into that big culvert at the back of the mouth? Or are Durhamites just particularly inept at brushing their teeth?

The Durham incidents seem to show no particular pattern, although alcohol was involved in two of the cases.

A 51-year-old man who tried to brush his teeth while drunk apparently just missed them and jammed the brush down his throat. The tip of the handle was still peeking from behind his tonsils when he got to the emergency room and doctors retrieved the apparatus with forceps. Obviously, the lesson here is that if you drink don't brush, and if you brush be careful of what you gargle.

A 60-year-old woman came to the hospital complaining of throat pain after having a seizure. The doctors found a toothbrush in her esophagus. She'd forgotten that she was brushing her teeth when the seizure struck.

A 20-year-old woman sucked down her toothbrush when she suffered a violent coughing spell while brushing. It went all the way to her stomach, and the doctors had to fish it out with a wire. (This must be a particularly satisfying activity to doctors, no doubt offering upon success a rush comparable to the one that comes when, after locking yourself out of your car, you finally manage to snag that little lock knob with a bent coat hanger that you have worked in around the window and manipulated with increasing frustration for an hour and a half.)

The final case was perhaps the strangest. After a weekend at the beach, a 19-year-old woman suffering from a severe hangover sought to relieve her nausea by tickling the back of her throat with a toothbrush to make herself throw up. In the process, she dropped her toothbrush, which went straight to her troubled stomach without accomplishing its purpose. Her nausea continued, the researchers reported, even after doctors had fetched back the toothbrush with a wire. The lesson here, I suppose, is that if you want to tickle your tonsils you should do it with something other than a toothbrush. Maybe a feather duster.

If I ever swallowed my toothbrush, I don't think I would be inclined to tell the truth about how it happened. That would be as embarrassing as trying to explain how you happened to have, say, a jelly bean up your nose. You can only come out of it looking foolish.

I'd either feign complete ignorance ("You found a toothbrush in my throat? Well, how on earth did that get there?), or I'd make up something completely outlandish ("See, I was just walking down the street, minding my own business, and this crazy guy screaming something that sounded like Russian comes running up with a gun and makes me swallow a toothbrush).

If through some harsh stroke of fate I should someday down a toothbrush, though, I'll try to make it to Durham to have it removed so that city can hold on to its hard-earned distinction, however difficult it may be to swallow.

Wooer's Arms and X-ray Skirts

"He Thinks He's a Dog Every April."

When was the last time you read a headline like that? I mean in a real newspaper, not one of those supermarket sleaze sheets?

I read that very headline on the front page of the *Atlanta Constitution* the other day. The story below it told about one W.H. Hedgepeth who jumped from a moving train while barking like a dog and snapping at fellow passengers. After being subdued, Hedgepeth said he had no control over his actions. He did the same thing every April just before his birthday, he explained, because his mother was attacked by a vicious dog shortly before his birth.

I wish I could tell you whether poor Hedgepeth was ever cured of his malady, but I can't. He's probably barking in heaven now, although not likely as a consequence of chasing cars. There weren't many cars around back in 1913 when that story appeared.

The April 29, 1913, edition was one of a stack of old *Constitutions* spanning a four-month period that an area resident found in the attic of her family home recently and allowed me to read. Let me tell you, if the *Constitution* is an example, newspapers sure were a lot livelier and more interesting in those days.

In July, for instance, was the tale of Esther Loos, 73, who escaped from a poorhouse in Poughkeepsie, N.Y., in the middle of the night to marry George Scofield, 55. Tracked down by authorities who sought to return her to the poorhouse, Esther fought back and was thrown into jail for resisting arrest.

I'll let the paper's account pick up the story from there: "It was a romantic elopement, Mrs. Scofield blushingly admitted through the bars of her cell. Scofield had whistled under her window three nights in succession and on the third night she could resist no longer. So packing up her few belongings, she climbed onto the porch from her window and slid down a post into her wooer's arms."

"Drunken Monkey Kills Dog Maims Master." That also occurred in July. The monkey bit off the hand of his owner, George Smith of Smithers, W.Va., and killed Smith's bulldog. This is what happened:

"Smith gave a party and the monkey had come in for his share of refreshments. After the guests departed, the monkey evinced a desire for another drink. Smith refused. The bulldog then sprang at the Simian, but the latter jumped on the dog's back and with his claws soon blinded him, then sank his teeth into the neck, killing him. Smith suffered his injuries in his efforts to subdue his pet."

Fashion was big in the news that summer. In an era when a flash of female ankle was considered scandalous, slit skirts and diaphanous dresses, which the papers were calling X-ray skirts, were just making their debut from Paris. Hardly a day passed without a front-page story about the daring new garments.

A young woman was arrested and sent to an asylum for wearing a slit skirt on the streets of Peoria, Ill. In Ayden, N.C., near Greenville, police beat back a mob of 100 men who pursued a young woman wearing a slit skirt that disclosed her stockinged calf. She was hustled into a millinery to have the skirt stitched.

At a baseball game in Norwalk, Conn., the disgusted manager of the Westports took his team off the field and defaulted after a young woman in an X-ray skirt distracted his outfielders by standing between them and the sun.

"Three flies were batted to the fence without the players making a move to intercept them," the report noted.

Slit skirts achieved some justification after an incident involving two women in Pittsburgh. Helen Brasmeth was able to escape the charge of a steer because her slit skirt allowed her to run, but her companion, Mrs. Harvey Wallace, "who wore one of the obsolete hobble gowns, not being able to do more than hop, went down and was trampled by the maddened animal."

If only I had the space, I would tell you the stories behind such headlines as these: "Took Needle From Foot, Uses It In Phonograph," "Oklahoma Pig Is Born With Elephant Trunk," "Dried Cantaloupe to Break Prune Monopoly," and "Mosquitoes Sing Doxology."

But I can't close without mentioning George Sanders, who was arrested near Freemont, Ohio, after "wandering like a wild man in the woods."

"He was laboring under a delusion that his wife had turned into a stump of a tree," the story said. It didn't mention whether anybody had bothered to check his wife to see if it might be true.

Just one more. It's about a guy in New Orleans who was arrested for trying to eat a four-foot steel beam. The arresting officer's attention was attracted to the man, according to the report, "by the sound of teeth on iron." The story closed with this additional bit of information: "Thrown into jail, he tried to eat the bars."